Cambridge Elements

Elements in Public and Nonprofit Administration
edited by
Robert Christensen
Brigham Young University
Jaclyn Piatak
University of North Carolina at Charlotte
Rosemary O'Leary
University of Kansas

DESIGN STRATEGIES IN PUBLIC SERVICES

Maria Cucciniello
Bocconi University

Greta Nasi
Bocconi University

Gregory Porumbescu
Rutgers University

Rosanna Tarricone
Bocconi University

Shaftesbury Road, Cambridge CB2 8EA, United Kingdom

One Liberty Plaza, 20th Floor, New York, NY 10006, USA

477 Williamstown Road, Port Melbourne, VIC 3207, Australia

314–321, 3rd Floor, Plot 3, Splendor Forum, Jasola District Centre, New Delhi – 110025, India

103 Penang Road, #05–06/07, Visioncrest Commercial, Singapore 238467

Cambridge University Press is part of Cambridge University Press & Assessment, a department of the University of Cambridge.

We share the University's mission to contribute to society through the pursuit of education, learning and research at the highest international levels of excellence.

www.cambridge.org
Information on this title: www.cambridge.org/9781009451741

DOI: 10.1017/9781009451734

© Maria Cucciniello, Greta Nasi, Gregory Porumbescu, and Rosanna Tarricone 2025

This publication is in copyright. Subject to statutory exception and to the provisions of relevant collective licensing agreements, with the exception of the Creative Commons version the link for which is provided below, no reproduction of any part may take place without the written permission of Cambridge University Press & Assessment.

An online version of this work is published at doi.org/10.1017/9781009451734 under a Creative Commons Open Access license CC-BY-NC 4.0 which permits re-use, distribution and reproduction in any medium for non-commercial purposes providing appropriate credit to the original work is given and any changes made are indicated. To view a copy of this license visit https://creativecommons.org/licenses/by-nc/4.0

When citing this work, please include a reference to the DOI 10.1017/9781009451734

First published 2025

A catalogue record for this publication is available from the British Library

ISBN 978-1-009-45174-1 Hardback
ISBN 978-1-009-45172-7 Paperback
ISSN 2515-4303 (online)
ISSN 2515-429X (print)

Cambridge University Press & Assessment has no responsibility for the persistence or accuracy of URLs for external or third-party internet websites referred to in this publication and does not guarantee that any content on such websites is, or will remain, accurate or appropriate.

For EU product safety concerns, contact us at Calle de José Abascal, 56, 1°, 28003 Madrid, Spain, or email eugpsr@cambridge.org

Design Strategies in Public Services

Elements in Public and Nonprofit Administration

DOI: 10.1017/9781009451734
First published online: December 2025

Maria Cucciniello
Bocconi University

Greta Nasi
Bocconi University

Gregory Porumbescu
Rutgers University

Rosanna Tarricone
Bocconi University

Author for correspondence: Maria Cucciniello,
maria.cucciniello@unibocconi.it

Abstract: This Element explores the transformative impact of integrating service design principles into public management and administration, championing a user-centred approach and co-design methodology. By reviewing existing literature, the authors define the scope and applications of service design within public administration and present three empirical studies to evaluate its implementation in public services. These studies reveal a trend towards embracing co-design and digital technologies, advancing a citizen-centred strategy for public service design. This approach prioritizes value creation and responsiveness, highlighting the importance of involving users and providers in the development of services that meet changing needs and promote inclusion. Combining theoretical insights with practical solutions, the Element offers a comprehensive framework for public management research. It highlights the need for ongoing engagement and integration of user experiences, presenting an effective strategy to navigate the complexities of public service design. This title is also available as Open Access on Cambridge Core.

Keywords: service design, user-centered approach, co-design, value creation, citizens.

© Maria Cucciniello, Greta Nasi, Gregory Porumbescu, and Rosanna Tarricone 2025

ISBNs: 9781009451741 (HB), 9781009451727 (PB), 9781009451734 (OC)
ISSNs: 2515-4303 (online), 2515-429X (print)

Contents

Introduction — 1

1 Understanding Service Design Theory for Improving Public Services — 2

2 The User-Centred Design Approach to Service Design — 10

3 Redesigning Municipal Services to Create City Value in the Aftermath of COVID-19 — 20

4 Embracing Citizen-Strategic Orientation in Public Service Design: The Application of the Double Diamond Design Process to Value Creation — 32

5 Engagement of Vulnerable Groups in Healthcare: Designing a Mobile Health Application to Promote Well-Being — 44

6 What Is Next for the Future of Public Service Design? — 59

References — 68

Introduction

Service design is a user-centred approach to creating and designing public services (Trischler et al., 2019). This approach is grounded in service design theory, which questions how the needs and experiences of users can be incorporated into the service design process to facilitate greater efficiency, effectiveness, and responsiveness. However, the application of service design to public service provision is still in its early stages. Therefore, this Cambridge Element contributes to public management research and practice by discussing how service design principles and tools can be leveraged to improve public service provision.

Despite the growing recognition of the importance of service design in public services, understanding of the links between service design, citizen engagement, and value creation is lacking – an issue that has moved to the forefront of the service design field (Andreassen et al., 2016). Moreover, the focus of service design has shifted from service design by experts towards service co-design with users (Trischler et al., 2018). Embedded within this shift is a focus upon value creation as the core element of service delivery. While early service management theory focused on service production and co-production, now the focus has moved to the use and consumption of services and the means through which services can add value to service users' lives (Vargo et al., 2008; Gronroos & Voima, 2013).

Current research on public service design mainly focuses on how to engage service users and embed their experiences in the decision-making processes that govern public service provision (Trischler et al., 2019; Trischler & Trischler, 2020). In this context, design strategies provide a disruptive solution to challenges commonly associated with engaging citizens. Service design theory is particularly relevant given its emphasis on a citizen orientation and its focus on empathy, thus enabling a deeper understanding of the challenges associated with public service provision and the context the service is being provided in. By grounding service design in a citizen orientation that emphasises value creation for service users, new and innovative solutions that align with the ideas and needs of all actors involved can be generated. Crucially, another important aspect of service design is that all proposed modifications are tested: to ensure their feasibility, the solutions are tested with small-scale prototypes that can be scaled up and diffused once validated. Therefore, design strategies and methodologies offer a novel, underutilised perspective on ways of leveraging user engagement to foster value-adding solutions to challenges associated with public service delivery.

Public services are complex, and their design must account for the needs of multiple stakeholders, including service users, service providers and policymakers. Acknowledging this complexity, this Element offers a distinctive approach to service design in public services by combining theoretical and practical perspectives. The theoretical lens draws from existing literature on public service logic and public service delivery to construct a conceptual framework. The practical perspective is enriched with diverse case studies across public service sectors that illustrate the tangible application of service design. Embracing a multidisciplinary stance, insights from public management, design science and social sciences converge to provide a holistic approach to service design. Adopting a user-centred design approach, the Elements places the needs and experiences of service users at the forefront of the design process.

In the sections that follow, we will provide an overview of service design research in public management and public administration, with a particular emphasis on user-centred approaches and tools for service design. Drawing on this conceptual baseline, we then provide three empirical studies that showcase innovative applications of service design in public services. These include redesigning municipal services post-COVID-19, improving satisfaction with public education, and developing a mobile health application to improve the well-being of patients with lung cancer. As we discuss, each study illustrates the importance of user-centred design approaches and tools, digital transformation, and the direct engagement of service users to enhance the value of public services. Additionally, we address the critical issue of inclusivity in service design, acknowledging potential biases favouring those with more resources, and offering specific, practical guidance on how to mitigate these challenges.

1 Understanding Service Design Theory for Improving Public Services

1.1 Definition and Evolution of Service Design Theory

The term *service design* emerged in the early 1980s to integrate the design of tangible products with the innovation of intangible service components – in effect, replacing unsystematic trial-and-error with a more deliberate, end-to-end logic. Shostack's seminal work (1982, 1984) framed this logic as a systematic planning exercise: every step in the service process should be mapped, tested, and iteratively refined so that each customer touchpoint delivers consistent value.

Building on this process view, Zomerdijk and Voss (2010) shifted attention from operational consistency to experience-centricity. They demonstrate that when designers understand the emotions, preferences, and desires that surface along the customer journey, they can deliberately script 'moments that matter', creating distinctive memories rather than merely efficient transactions.

As digital channels proliferated, Glushko (2010) widened the lens again, classifying service interactions as person-to-person, person-to-machine, or machine-to-machine. This triad acknowledges that technology is now a co-actor in service delivery; designing smooth hand-offs among people and smart devices has become as critical as choreographing face-to-face encounters.

Kimbell (2011) then reconceptualised service design as an exploratory, open-ended inquiry. Instead of following a linear blueprint, designers are encouraged to embrace uncertainty, prototype early, and iterate often – an approach that keeps the process responsive to emergent user insights.

Recognising that experiences unfold in concrete settings, Secomandi and Snelders (2011) foreground the service interface: the blend of material artefacts, physical environments, and embodied human interactions that mediate every encounter. Their holistic perspective reminds us that the tangible and intangible are inseparable in practice.

Andreassen et al. (2016) translate these ideas into a managerial agenda, positioning service design as a vehicle for customer-centric transformation. By systematically surfacing and addressing user needs, organisations can boost satisfaction and loyalty while gaining operational insight.

Finally, Karpen et al. (2017) highlight the capabilities and culture required to sustain such efforts. Design thinking must permeate everyday routines, and cross-functional collaboration must be institutionalised if service design is to move beyond isolated projects and influence strategic direction.

Together, these contributions chart a progression – from systematic planning, to immersive experience crafting, to technology-mediated interactions, and finally to organisational capability building. This trajectory reveals service design as both a *method* (how to map and improve service processes) and a *mindset* (how to embed user-centred, exploratory thinking across the organisation). The next subsection builds on this foundation by examining how these principles extend to service design in the context of public service logic, demonstrating the continued evolution of service design in contemporary contexts.

1.2 Service Design in the Context of Public Service Logic

Research in the field of services provides important perspectives for public administration and management, contributing to the conceptual advancement within the developing Public Service Logic (PSL) (Hardyman et al., 2019; Mills et al., 2023; Strokosch & Osborne, 2023). Early service research distinguished services from tangible goods, highlighting consumer participation due to the distinctive characteristics of services – intangibility, inseparability, perishability, and heterogeneity (Zeithaml et al., 1985; Nankervis et al., 2005; Grönroos, 2016; Johnston et al., 2020).

A foundational influence on this evolution has been the development of Service-Dominant Logic (S-D Logic) by Vargo and Lusch (2004, 2008, 2016), which reconceptualised service as the application of operant resources (e.g. skills and knowledge) for the benefit of others and positioned value as co-created by multiple actors rather than delivered unilaterally. S-D Logic introduced a shift from goods-dominant perspectives to a framework where service (singular) is the basis of all exchange, with key axioms including: service as the fundamental basis of exchange, actors as resource integrators, and value as phenomenologically determined by the beneficiary. These principles laid critical groundwork for PSL by foregrounding co-creation, actor interdependence, and the contextual nature of value (Vargo & Lusch, 2017).

The transition towards a service logic in public administration, as advocated by Osborne and Strokosch (2013), builds on and adapts these foundational ideas to the public sector context. PSL focuses on public services not as tangible products but as platforms for co-creating value through diverse user experiences (Hardyman et al., 2019; Osborne, 2020; Strokosch & Osborne, 2020; Osborne et al., 2022a; Osborne et al., 2024). For instance, Osborne (2020) emphasises that public service delivery does not involve ownership transfer, but rather is an intangible, relational process aimed at generating public value. Public services are characterised by user participation, shared responsibility, and context-dependent value, contrasting with the standardised, consumption-oriented model typical of manufactured goods (Osborne et al., 2013).

This conceptual convergence between S-D Logic and PSL underscores that value in public services emerges through lived experiences, interactions, and institutional arrangements – echoing S-D Logic's focus on service ecosystems and value-in-context (Vargo & Lusch, 2008, 2016). It also reinforces that PSL is not a departure from but rather a contextual extension of S-D Logic, adapted to the governance, ethical, and institutional complexity of public services.

Bridging this discussion with the evolution of service design methodologies reveals a natural progression in how services are conceptualised and delivered. The emphasis on user experiences and interactions aligns with service design's commitment to user-centredness, creativity, and empathy (Simon, 1969; Bason, 2017; Bason, 2017; McGann et al., 2018). Service design processes extend value co-creation principles by actively integrating the diverse knowledge, needs, and social contexts of service users into design and delivery. In doing so, service design reinforces the foundational S-D Logic notion that value emerges through collaborative, contextual, and dynamic engagements among actors within service ecosystems.

This integrative approach enriches both service design and PSL by emphasising that public value is not merely delivered but co-constituted through continuous, reciprocal interaction among diverse stakeholders.

Service design has attracted scholarly attention since the 1970s and has since emerged as a distinctive paradigm challenging expert-driven design methodologies (Simon, 1969; Bason, 2017; Bason, 2017). Traditional approaches, emphasising instrumental rationality and expert knowledge, are contrasted by service design methodologies that prioritise creativity, curiosity and empathy, particularly through human-centredness, problem-solving, testing, and iteration (McGann et al., 2018).The scholarly literature on service design in public sector organisations reveals *a growing interest in enhancing public services through innovative design approaches*. Human-centred design (HCD) has gained prominence as a valuable framework for addressing the evolving needs of citizens and stakeholders in the public sector (Brown, 2008) and widely adopted in public service innovation, particularly in public service innovation, due to its emphasis on empathy, user involvement, and iterative development (Björgvinsson et al., 2012; Bason, 2017). The approach typically unfolds in phases – inspiration (understanding user needs), ideation (generating and prototyping solutions), and implementation (delivering and scaling interventions). In public service settings, HCD supports inclusive innovation by foregrounding empathy, user voice, and iterative learning (Bason, 2010; Björgvinsson et al., 2012).

Researchers stress the importance of understanding the unique challenges of the public sector when applying service design principles (Meroni & Sangiorgi, 2011). To this end, service design in the public sector involves *improving efficiency and fostering citizen engagement and satisfaction* (Mulgan et al., 2007). The integration of *co-creation methods*, where citizens actively participate in the design process, is identified as a key element in achieving more responsive and inclusive public services (Alves et al., 2016). Additionally, the literature highlights the role of *digital technologies* in augmenting service design efforts within the public sector (Haug et al., 2023). E-government initiatives, incorporating service design principles, aim to leverage information and communication technologies for more accessible, transparent and user-friendly public services (Chun et al., 2010; Cucciniello et al., 2017). Building on the aforementioned points, service design has evolved from focusing solely on the delivery of predefined, functional services to shaping the broader servicescape – the physical, social, and institutional environment in which services are experienced and co-created (Bitner, 1992; Wetter-Edman et al., 2014; Sangiorgi & Prendiville, 2017).

This emphasises the creation of positive experiences for those interacting with services, transcending immediate user needs to consider long-term impacts on users' lives and societal transformation (Patrício et al., 2008; Kimbell, 2011; van Buuren et al., 2020). Service design achieves this goal by investigating stakeholders' interactions, experiences and values through a methodology underpinned by the principles of openness, participation and inclusivity (Schwoerer et al., 2022).

A key to design methodologies within the PSL framework is to embed user-centredness throughout problem identification, understanding, and solution development in iterative processes (Wetter-Edman et al., 2014). Accordingly, two approaches within service design, the informational and inspirational approaches, present different perspectives on how to embed user-centredness in the design process. The informational approach focuses on uncovering service users' needs through scientific research, relying on principles of reliability, validity and rigor (Howlett et al., 2015). In contrast, the inspirational approach roots itself in experimentation, focusing on ambiguity and generating future-focused solutions exemplified by policy or living labs (Sanders, 2005; van Buuren et al., 2020).

The emphasis on participation and inclusion within service design holds particular relevance to public services, where collectiveness is fundamental to participatory processes and outcomes. Yet, despite the promises of innovation and a user-centred approach, challenges persist regarding the practical implementation of service design in the public sector. For example, some argue that existing attempts to apply service design principles are reductionary, focusing on constituent parts while neglecting the broader service ecosystem, which, in turn, may limit the transformative potential of this approach to public service design (Howlett, 2014; Vink et al., 2021a).

Moreover, questions arise as to whether public service organisations (PSOs) can fully embrace quick and iterative problem-solving approaches, given not only the sector's perceived aversion to risk (Alves et al., 2016) but also the significant legal and procedural constraints they operate under. It is not simply a matter of risk aversion or inertia; many PSOs must adhere to strict due process requirements, including transparency, accountability, and fairness, which limit their capacity for rapid iteration. In some jurisdictions, public sector decisions are subject to judicial review, adding yet another layer of complexity and caution to their operations (Christensen & Laegreid, 2007). Therefore, while service design principles that promote iteration can be beneficial, they must be adapted to align with the institutional and legal frameworks governing PSOs. The challenge lies in balancing innovation with the need to uphold these obligations, ensuring that any iteration is careful and deliberate rather than rapid and flexible.

In view of these challenges, scholars emphasise the need for a nuanced understanding of the organisational and cultural factors influencing its successful implementation in the public sector (Gascó-Hernández & Torres, 2015). Furthermore, the measurement of outcomes and impacts remains a subject of ongoing research, with scholars exploring methodologies to assess the effectiveness of service design interventions in achieving their intended objectives (Demunter et al., 2019). Building upon this foundation, a recent study by Strokosch and Osborne (2023) delves deeper into the application and implications of design approaches in public service settings. The authors carefully explore the focus and impact of design practice, marking a pivotal investigation into how human-centred design is operationalised within PSOs and its consequent effects on public service delivery (Strokosch & Osborne, 2023).

Ongoing research explores methodologies for evaluating outcomes and demonstrating the tangible benefits of adopting design principles in public service contexts. In summary, the scholarly literature on public service design underscores the significance of citizen-centric approaches, co-creation strategies, and the integration of digital technologies. Successful implementation requires attention to organisational and cultural factors, and ongoing efforts focus on refining evaluation methods to demonstrate the effectiveness and impact of public service design interventions.

1.3 Engagement as a Key Element of Service Design

Service design theory offers important insights for theory and practice as it creates a framework organisations can use to better understand and meet the evolving needs and expectations of their customers. Specifically, applying a service design approach allows those designing public services to uncover insights about customer preferences, pain points, and desires, which can then be used to create more meaningful and impactful services. Additionally, as service ecosystems become increasingly complex and interconnected, having a holistic understanding of how +different elements interact and influence each other is crucial for successful service innovation. From this perspective, service design theory is essential to service innovation because it brings ideas to life and creates a foundation for progress towards overall better services that more accurately and efficiently meet users' needs.

These diverse perspectives demonstrate the evolution of service design theory from a basic approach to providing services towards a more experience- and user-centred framework. Today, service design theory is crucial due to its role in driving service innovation and value co-creation within service ecosystems. As service design has grown to be a user-centred, collaborative, and holistic approach, it has become instrumental in improving existing services and creating new ones. Embracing service design theory through a multidisciplinary lens has become a strategic imperative for both service researchers and practitioners.

1.4 Unveiling the Potential of Service Design for Value Co-Creation in Public Services

By framing public services as intricate ecosystems that integrate diverse resources, service design transcends the conventional focus on individual services to emphasise the overarching constructs of experience and context. Crucially, focusing on value co-creation processes serves as an important foundation for institutional change by incorporating the knowledge, skills, and backgrounds of diverse actors. Relatedly, this approach to designing public services acknowledges that services, even when carefully designed, undergo continuous adjustments. Applying design principles in public service contexts can significantly enhance the co-creation of value, provided there is a deep understanding of how various resources within a complex ecosystem integrate (Vargo & Lusch, 2016; Grönroos, 2019; Strokosch & Osborne, 2023). This approach shifts the focus from the *provision of services* to fostering *service experiences* and understanding the context in which these services are delivered (Jaakkola et al., 2015; Schwoerer et al., 2022). Recognising the processes of value co-creation is crucial for initiating the institutional changes needed to achieve the benefits associated with service design.

The term 'Service' refers to a value creation perspective, distinct from 'services', which denotes a specific product category requiring different design, production, and delivery approaches (Edvardsson et al., 2005). In SDL and SL, 'Service' represents the process of doing something beneficial with and for other actors, where value is co-created during use rather than produced and delivered as a finished product (Vargo & Lusch, 2008, 2016). Thus, value is co-created and context-dependent, shaped by the beneficiary's experience and the social setting (Edvardsson et al., 2011). The following subsections further differentiate 'service' from 'services' by tracing key conceptual developments in SL and SDL, establishing the foundational elements of the service lens.

Service design captures the subjective and social dimensions of service, including the unique contributions of individuals' knowledge, skills, and backgrounds. However, regardless of the initial design, services will inevitably be adjusted to meet the evolving needs and experiences of users, particularly in fields like education and healthcare, where empathy, equity, and fairness are paramount.

The design process, adjustments, and resulting value are influenced by the service context, including institutional norms, societal values, and user expectations.

By prioritising experience and context, designing for service acknowledges the multifaceted nature of the value co-creation process.

Our contribution builds on and extends the PSL framework by clarifying the distinctions between 'services' as discrete offerings and 'service' as a dynamic, co-creative process, aligning with Trischler et al. (2023) in advancing a more nuanced understanding of value co-creation within public service contexts. We contend that service design, woven into the fabric of interactions, plays a pivotal role in influencing design processes, service outputs, and the entire spectrum of service delivery. This holistic impact underscores the potential of service design to shape and enhance value accrual in the dynamic landscape of public services.

Service design theory offers valuable insights for the public sector that extend beyond the realm of service design. In the realm of public services, service design emerges as a pivotal strategy for value creation, aligning with the principles of PSL. Rooted in user-centredness, service design transcends traditional, product-centric approaches prevalent in the twentieth-century New Public Management (NPM) framework. Unlike the latter's focus on internal efficiency and individual entities, service design's methodology is built upon creativity, curiosity, and empathy. This paradigm shift emphasises the design of the 'servicescape' to not only satisfy immediate user needs but also create positive experiences that extend to long-term impacts on users' lives and societal transformation.

Through participatory and inclusive practices, service design engages stakeholders in the public context, going beyond mere consultation to active co-design with citizens and service users. Service design's emphasis on openness, participation, and inclusivity reflects a commitment to understanding and incorporating diverse perspectives, which is crucial for addressing complex social goals inherent in public service organisations. Despite challenges and cautions about implementation, service design in the public sector has the potential to foster innovation and an outcomes-focused approach, ultimately contributing to the creation of enduring societal value.

Service design theory plays a pivotal role in reimagining public services through its use of a user-centred approach and its emphasis on leveraging design principles to meet the dynamic needs and expectations of users, thereby acting as a catalyst for creating enduring societal value.

In summary, this section underscored the essential role of service design theory in understanding and improving public services. The adoption of a user-centred approach and the incorporation of design principles empower organisations to enhance service quality and encourage active citizen participation. Thus, service design theory, with its valuable insights and innovative frameworks, becomes a catalyst for creating services that align with the evolving needs and expectations of users.

2 The User-Centred Design Approach to Service Design

2.1 How Are Services Designed in the Public Sphere?

This section delves into the pivotal role of service design in fostering value creation, with a special focus on engaging citizens through innovative methodologies and exploring essential principles supporting service design adoption and implementation (Downe, 2020). Central to this discussion is the application of the Double Diamond design process, a key feature of service design theory that underscores the importance of validating the need for a service before delving into its development to ensure it meets the users' and organisations' requirements.

The transformative impact of service design, especially evident during the pandemic's shift towards digital business models, illustrates its critical role in addressing contemporary challenges. In some cases, this period also sparked conversations around sustainability, though these shifts were less uniform.

It underscores the necessity for service researchers to anticipate and mitigate unintended consequences, such as exclusions and environmental impacts, through collaborative efforts with public sector organisations, healthcare, non-profits, and design firms. This section proposes that the iterative nature of service design is essential for not only developing services that meet user needs but also emphasising the significance of service design in the creation of value through citizen engagement. Co-design actively involves citizens/service users and draws on their past experiences to generate fresh ideas and support improvement and innovation (Donetto et al., 2015; Schwoerer et al., 2022). Citizens/service users are invited to actively contribute as an essential resource throughout the design process, including idea generation and the development of solutions (Wetter-Edman et al., 2014). Subsequently, there has been a discernible upswing in the utilisation of explicit co-design principles in public services over the past decade, with a growing number of applications grounded in the concept of co-design for value creation (Blomkamp, 2018; Dudau et al., 2019; Nasi & Choi, 2023). Exploring the impacts of power differentials on co-design (Farr, 2018) and delineating the linkages between co-design and social innovation (Voorberg et al., 2015; Whicher & Trick, 2019) have emerged as pivotal themes in this evolutionary trajectory.

2.2 The Double Diamond: A Framework for Iterative and Inclusive Service Design

The Double Diamond design process originating from the Design Council in 2004 serves as a conceptual model elucidating the overarching stages traversed by numerous design innovation initiatives. This approach, notably adopted by the Scottish Government, emphasises an ethnographic methodology that draws heavily from service design theories, including the use of personas and other tools as key instruments for enhancing citizen engagement (Design Council, 2007; Scottish Government, 2019): 'The design process reminds us that we have to be sure we're creating the right thing before we can design something that's fit for purpose and meets the needs of users, staff, or organisations' (Scottish Government, 2019, p. 14).

The Double Diamond *is a visual representation of the design and innovation process. It's a simple way to describe the steps taken in any design and innovation project, irrespective of methods and tools used* (https://www.design council.org.uk*)*.

The service design adopted by the Design Council presents a perspicuous, comprehensive and visually intuitive representation of the design process. Since its inception in 2004, the Double Diamond has garnered global recognition, with an extensive online repository of supporting research.

The Design Council's utilisation of the Double Diamond effectively communicates a design process accessible to both experts in service design and non-experts. The two diamonds represent a sequential progression involving the expansive exploration of an issue (divergent thinking) followed by a focus on specific actions (convergent thinking). It is organised into the following four phases.

Divergent thinking characterises the Discover and Develop stages, encouraging designers to explore broadly whether to understand user needs and contextual dynamics in the Discover phase or to generate a wide range of possible solutions in the Develop phase (Brown, 2008; Dorst, 2011). Convergent thinking, by contrast, underpins the Define and Deliver stages, where designers analyse and synthesise insights to clearly frame the problem and subsequently refine the most promising ideas into actionable solutions (Kimbell, 2011; Bason, 2017). This structured oscillation between expansion and narrowing supports creativity while maintaining strategic focus, making the Double Diamond particularly valuable in complex service contexts.

Discover (Exploration): This is the first phase of the Double Diamond process. It involves open-ended exploration and research. During this phase, designers seek to understand the users' needs, motivations, and behaviours.

This involves gathering insights and perspectives from a wide range of sources to fully comprehend the problem or challenge at hand. Techniques such as user interviews, observations, and focus groups are typically employed. The goal is to gather as much information and as many insights as possible without immediately seeking solutions.

Define (Creation): In this phase, the focus shifts from exploration to synthesising the gathered information to define the core problem(s) that need to be solved. This involves analysing the data collected in the Discover phase and identifying patterns, trends, and insights. Designers aim to articulate the problem clearly and succinctly, often in the form of a problem statement or a design brief. This phase is critical as it sets the direction for ideation by providing a clear and focused problem to solve.

Develop (Reflection): Here, the process opens up again into a phase of ideation and conceptualisation. With a clear understanding of the defined problem, designers begin to generate a range of ideas and potential solutions. This phase encourages creativity and the exploration of many different possibilities, using techniques like brainstorming, sketching, and prototype development. The aim is to explore a wide variety of solutions without immediately judging or dismissing them.

Deliver (Implementation): The final phase focuses on refining and testing the developed ideas to deliver effective solutions. It involves selecting the most promising ideas from the Develop phase and transforming them into practical and viable solutions. This often includes creating prototypes, conducting user testing, and iteratively improving the solutions based on feedback. The Deliver phase culminates in the final solution that can be implemented or launched.

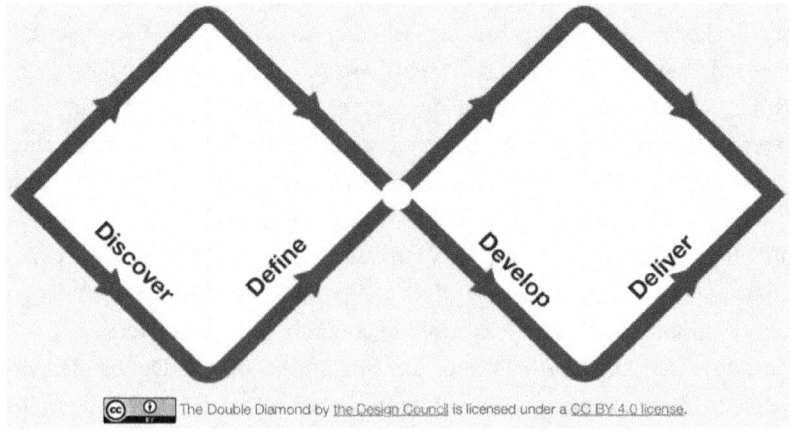

Figure 1 The Double Diamond

Throughout the Double Diamond, the emphasis is on moving from a broad understanding of a problem space (diverging) to a focused and actionable solution (converging), thus ensuring a thorough exploration and validation of ideas and solutions. The process is inherently non-linear, a characteristic illustrated through the directional arrows present in Figure 1. Various organisations have observed that this approach often facilitates the uncovering of profound insights into fundamental issues, compelling a cyclical return to the formative stages of the process. The initiation and evaluation of preliminary ideas are integral components of the discovery phase, reflecting the principle that within the constantly evolving digital milieu, the concept of a 'completed' idea is obsolete. Feedback on the efficacy of services is systematically solicited and employed in an iterative cycle of enhancement based on the insights provided.

The Double Diamond can be used to navigate through a comprehensive process that encompasses the identification of needs, articulation of problems, formulation, and evaluation of solutions and the achievement of tangible outcomes and value. This process orchestrates user engagement, thus facilitating a fluid transition between the expansive exploration of broad concepts and the focused refinement of specific solutions. The construct of the first diamond serves a pivotal role in guiding the identification of the most pertinent challenges, ensuring a thorough comprehension of end-user requirements. Following this, the second diamond provides a structured framework for the design, enhancement, and realisation of the envisioned solutions, employing prototyping, and testing with both end-users and service providers to validate and refine the solutions.

The Double Diamond underscores the essence of service design as a dynamic and iterative process that is not merely focused on the creation of products and services but also dedicated to the cultivation of meaningful and impactful experiences that resonate with the complex and changing needs of users and stakeholders.

2.3 Placing the User's Experience at the Heart of Public Service Delivery

This subsection discusses various service design methods employed for gathering information crucial to the development of public service system designs. Specifically, the focus is on assessing the efficacy of these methods in addressing the dual challenges of managing the complexities within service systems and comprehending user experiences. Drawing on established literature (e.g. Bitner et al., 1990; Edvardsson & Roos, 2001), we explore the application and effectiveness of some prominent service design techniques commonly employed in service design projects (Kimbell & Seidel, 2008; Diana et al., 2009; Segelström, 2009; Stickdorn & Schneider, 2010; Zomerdijk & Voss,

2010). Additionally, given their widespread usage in service design, a detailed analysis of these service design techniques is presented. To establish a foundation for the analysis, in this context, a service is defined as 'something that assists individuals in accomplishing their necessary tasks' (Down, 2020).

Drawing on research by Trischler and Scott (2015), Trischler et al. (2019) and Popli and Rishi (2021), it is imperative to prioritise the user's experience in public service delivery. This entails embracing service design methods and frameworks that actively involve users as co-producers.

Service design employs a broad array of tools and methodologies to create and improve services that cater to the intricate requirements of users and stakeholders alike (Stickdorn & Schneider, 2010). This vast toolkit encompasses various approaches, each designed to tackle distinct aspects of service design, from understanding user needs to prototyping and testing service concepts. In this subsection, we will introduce only a select few of these tools, focusing on the most popular and widely adopted approaches to service design (Kimbell & Seidel, 2008; Diana et al., 2009; Segelström, 2009; Stickdorn & Schneider, 2010; Zomerdijk & Voss, 2010). These methodologies, such as end user persona development, customer journey mapping, and service blueprints, are fundamental in facilitating a deep understanding of the service experience, allowing service design scholars and designers to craft solutions that are both innovative and user-centred. By employing these tools, a holistic and empathetic approach to developing services that genuinely meet the needs and expectations of their users can be ensured.

Persona development: The persona development concept, rooted in human-computer interaction research, emerges as a crucial mechanism for translating abstract customer segments into considerations based on individual perspectives. Defined by Cooper (1999) as 'fictitious, specific, and concrete representations of target users', underscoring that their development is grounded in research rather than arbitrary invention, personas furnish a memorable and actionable framework. Personas are based on composite archetypes and help designers empathise with users' needs, behaviours, and motivations (Pruitt & Adlin, 2006; Stickdorn et al., 2018). While demographic details such as age or occupation may provide contextual grounding, effective personas prioritise psychographic attributes such as attitudes, goals, frustrations, capabilities, and behavioural patterns – because these factors shape how users experience and interact with services (Goodwin, 2009). Emphasising psychographics allows personas to capture the lived realities of service users and support the design of experiences that are both meaningful and context-sensitive. Personas serve as an invaluable resource for concentrating on the primary user by elucidating behaviour patterns and pinpointing user needs. The utility of personas extends beyond this focus, facilitating communication among stakeholders, informing decision-making processes, and providing a basis for evaluating concepts, as acknowledged by both academics and professionals (Pruitt & Adlin, 2006; Mulder & Yaar, 2007). They assimilate contextual information pertinent to service challenges, capturing the requirements, needs, or desires typically associated with the persona, and are enriched with 'softer' details like personality traits to offer a more nuanced and personalised portrayal. The crafting of personas is fundamental in making the abstract notion of user bases tangible, thereby facilitating empathy and tailored engagement with specific user segments. Through the integration of demographic, psychographic, and behavioural insights, personas act as a guiding structure, enriching the process of developing solutions that resonate with user needs and expectations. Most personas are developed from research insights which are usually gathered from interviews and focus groups (Stickdorn & Schneider, 2011).

Personas help designers understand the diverse needs, behaviours, motivations, and challenges of different segments of the population. They are a design tool used to construct representative archetypes of the intended user groups for whom a service is being developed (Pruitt & Adlin, 2006; Cooper et al., 2014). To ensure their effectiveness, personas must be grounded in empirical research and crafted to reflect the diversity, inclusivity, and variability of real users' experiences, avoiding stereotypes, and oversimplification (Goodwin, 2009; Stickdorn et al., 2018).

Here is an example of its application to the redesign of a Municipality Social Service Website. Imagine a local government wanting to redesign its online social services portal, which offers resources for employment, housing assistance, healthcare, and more. The portal is currently difficult to navigate, resulting in underutilisation by residents who need these services most. To improve the portal, the government could apply the personas methodology. Firstly, it is essential to gather data about the residents who use (or need to use) the social services portal. This could include an assessment of the user behaviours of the current website. To map needs and perceptions of satisfaction, it could also include assessments based on surveys and interviews with residents and users as well as focus groups with key population segments (e.g. seniors, low-income families, people with disabilities) as well as meetings with social service workers and community advocates.

Based on this research, it is possible to create a set of personas that represent the different types of users who will interact with the portal. Here are three examples of personas that could be used in this context such as a single mother named Mary, a retired citizen named John and Saman a recent immigrant with physical disability. For each of them it is important to depict their profile (e.g. Mary is a single mother of two, working a part-time job while juggling childcare. She has minimal free time and limited access to the internet, relying on her smartphone for most online services); goals (e.g. Mary wants quick access to housing assistance and affordable childcare services); challenges (e.g. Mary struggles with complex forms, lengthy application processes, and finding specific information on the portal. She often abandons the process halfway through because of time constraints) and needs (e.g. a mobile-friendly, easy-to-navigate interface with simple, clear instructions, and the ability to save applications to complete later).

Using these personas, the design team makes informed decisions about the portal's layout, content, and features that can be tested with a small group of users representing each persona. Feedback is gathered, and adjustments are made to improve the service, ensuring it meets the community's real needs

Customer journey mapping: Customer journey mapping is a vital tool that helps visualise user interactions and experiences throughout the service journey. It emphasises active stakeholder involvement in identifying pain points and areas for improvement, ultimately leading to user-centred design decisions. Furthermore, Customer journey mapping encourages cross-functional collaboration, thereby fostering alignment among stakeholders by establishing a shared comprehension of the service ecosystem. Visualising and mapping techniques play a crucial role in rendering service systems and processes more transparent. They clarify which components of the service system impact the overall user experience (Patricio et al., 2011). The relevance of customer journey mapping is underscored by its ability to comprehensively capture the user's experience throughout their journey and highlight the 'touchpoints' within the service system (Zomerdijk & Voss, 2010). Active involvement of consumers in the analysis and design processes, as advocated by Sanders and Stappers (2008) and Ostrom et al. (2010), is essential for fully integrating user experiences and gaining valuable insights. *Collaborative design workshops* have been effectively employed as part of these visualisation and mapping techniques to facilitate participants' sharing of their experiences and the generation of innovative concepts (Bason, 2010; Steen et al., 2011).

For example, in redesigning an unemployment benefits service, a journey map follows a user like Rachel, who is a typical persona (e.g. she is a 45-year-old office worker who has just lost her job). The key stages in Lena's journey to access unemployment benefits are identified as follows: awareness (e.g. Learning about the unemployment benefits programme); application (e.g. Applying for benefits); approval/denial, receiving benefits and reintegration (e.g. using resources to find new employment). Through customer journey mapping, the service designer understands the challenges she faces in accessing the service, such as difficult-to-find information, complex forms, long waiting times, and unclear payment processes. The map leads to improvements like clearer information architecture, simplified application forms, better communication, and integration with job placement services.

Service blueprinting: A service blueprint is a visual and systematic representation of a service that helps organisations comprehensively analyse and design service processes. It maps out the entire service journey, illustrating customer interactions, frontstage activities, backstage processes, and support systems involved in service delivery. This blueprinting process is crucial for identifying potential pain points, improving efficiency, and enhancing the overall customer experience. As described by Shostack (1984), a pioneer in service blueprinting, it is a method to 'chart the sequence of events and interactions in a service process'. This involves delineating customer actions, frontstage and backstage processes, support processes, and physical evidence encountered during service delivery. Bitner et al. (2008) emphasise service blueprinting as a 'practical technique for service innovation', highlighting its *utility in fostering innovation and improving service design.* The technique aids in identifying touchpoints, understanding customer emotions, and aligning various components to deliver a seamless and efficient service. Service blueprinting serves as a valuable tool for organisations to visually map and analyse their service processes, leading to enhanced service delivery and customer satisfaction. It helps to reveal the process behind critical service elements that define the user experience (Stickdorn & Schneider, 2011).

2.3.1 Exploratory and Confirmatory Focus Groups

Building on the methodological foundation presented thus far, we also include Tremblay and colleagues' (2010) framework based on exploratory and confirmatory focus groups (EFGs and CFGs, respectively) as it presents a robust methodology that has been widely used over the past years for the refinement of artefact design. It can also be adapted for service design, particularly in the context of re-designing services. This adaptation leverages the iterative nature of EFGs and the validating strength of CFGs to enhance the user-centred design process, ensuring that services not only meet user expectations but also enhance user experiences in meaningful ways.

In their original development in design research (Tremblay et al., 2010a), EFGs serve to provide critical feedback that informs modifications of the artefact under study, while CFGs are used to demonstrate the utility of the artefact design in the application field.

Exploration and Creation Phase

In the realm of service design, EFGs can be utilised to gather in-depth insights into users' experiences with existing services. This phase involves engaging with users to explore their perceptions, frustrations, and needs regarding a service. These discussions are pivotal for the following:

- Uncovering insights: Facilitating the discovery of broad themes and users motivations
- Identifying service gaps: Highlighting areas where the current service may fall short in meeting user expectations or needs.
- Gathering contextual understanding: Providing a deeper look into the environmental and personal factors that influence user interactions with the service. In particular, the qualitative data gathered during these sessions are crucial to construct personas and generate hypotheses about how a service can be re-designed to better cater to its users.

The objective here is to uncover latent needs and opportunities for innovation that may not be immediately evident. Researchers can then synthesise these insights to propose tangible improvements or entirely new service concepts. This exploratory and creative phase is inherently iterative, with each session potentially unveiling new directions for refinement. Thus, through successive EFGs, a comprehensive understanding of user needs and service gaps can be developed, thereby guiding the subsequent design or re-design process.

Reflection and Implementation Phase

Following the exploration phase, CFGs are crucial for assessing the practical utility and user acceptance of the proposed service changes in real-world settings and for creating further ideas. The CFG participants are exposed to the re-designed service, either in prototype form or through detailed service blueprints, to evaluate its effectiveness, usability, and overall appeal. These focus groups should be structured to capture qualitative feedback on user experiences of specific aspects of the service design. These sessions are key to the following:

- Testing re-design concepts: Validating whether the re-design ideas resonate with the target audience and address the issues identified in the exploratory phase.
- Refining service propositions: Ensuring that the modifications proposed accurately reflect the user's needs and align with their expectations.
- Closing feedback loops: Identifying any overlooked elements in the re-design process and ensuring all user segments are adequately considered.

In Section 4 we use this methodology to help redesign the education services taking into account the feedback and the organisational analysis.

Running multiple CFGs with experientially distinct participant groups – such as a focus group of single mothers, another of retirees, or immigrants – enables the collection of diverse viewpoints, thereby enhancing the reliability and inclusiveness of the findings.

Adapting Tremblay and colleagues' (2010b) approach to service design necessitates a flexible, yet systematic, process. Initial exploratory sessions should focus on understanding the user's interaction with the service-identifying pain points and unmet needs. Insights from these sessions would then inform the development or refinement of service prototypes, which are then subjected to CFGs for validation. This cycle may be repeated several times, with each iteration refining the service design based on feedback until it meets the criteria for successful implementation in the field.

2.4 Benefits of Service Design Tools for Designing Public Services

The use of persona development, customer journey mapping, service blueprints, and focus groups in service design underscores their pivotal roles in achieving the following:

- *User-centred design*: Both persona development and customer journey mapping champion a user-centred ethos, instilling empathy among designers and stakeholders (Brown, 2008).
- *Holistic service understanding*: The fusion of personas and journey maps engenders a holistic grasp of the service ecosystem. This comprehensive perspective empowers public managers and scholars to tackle challenges across various touchpoints, culminating in more effective service design (Meroni & Sangiorgi, 2011).
- *Enhanced collaboration:* These tools act as catalysts for collaboration among cross-functional teams, providing a shared visual lexicon and unified comprehension of user requirements (Junginger & Sangiorgi, 2009).
- *Bias mitigation*: When intentionally applied to reflect structurally disadvantaged user groups, such as low-income individuals or digitally excluded populations, these tools help surface inequities and design barriers, enabling practitioners to develop services that are more inclusive and less biased toward users with greater resources (Steen et al., 2011; Le Dantec & Fox, 2015).

The tools and processes presented in this section are indispensable cornerstones of service design. They offer a structured, user-focused framework for crafting and enhancing services, and their integration forms a robust foundation for designing services that resonate with users, nurture empathy, and navigate the intricacies of the service landscape. As service design continues to evolve, these tools retain their fundamental role in shaping impactful services for users.

2.4.1 Service Design in Practice

In the following sections, we examine insights drawn from three distinct public service design projects that actively engaged users. These projects, set within the context of complex service systems, demonstrate the unique yet crucial role of service users as co-producers within these systems. Additionally, they highlight key actions that enhance the manageability of service systems while providing a concrete illustration of the service design methodology in practice. This exploration offers a deeper understanding of effective strategies for involving users in public service design endeavours. Furthermore, we address the critical issue of inclusivity in service design, acknowledging the potential biases favouring those with greater resources and offering practical guidance on how to mitigate these challenges. Collectively, these case studies contribute to the ongoing discourse framed by Public Service Logic (PSL) (see Osborne, 2010; Osborne et al., 2013; Radnor et al., 2015).

3 Redesigning Municipal Services to Create City Value in the Aftermath of COVID-19

The reverberation of the global pandemic has guided cities into an era of adaptation, compelling them to embrace new ways of living while grappling with the multifaceted challenges posed by the economic crisis. This juncture presents a unique opportunity to craft a long-term value proposition that transcends immediate hurdles as the pandemic-induced norms of social distancing, limited access to physical spaces and other COVID-19 restrictions have necessitated a profound re-evaluation of how citizens interact with institutions and service providers.

Furthermore, governments at various levels have found themselves contending with a slew of complex issues, ranging from economic and health concerns to welfare problems, unemployment, and a decline in competitiveness. These challenges have had a particularly pronounced impact on local governments, with some struggling to adapt to the evolving landscape. Certain local authorities continue to rely on fragmented, non-digitised processes, placing additional coordination burdens on citizens seeking essential services. Recognising that municipal resources alone may prove insufficient to drive recovery and long-term economic development within the confines of traditional government-citizen dynamics, this case study helped identify solutions that empower municipalities to adapt their city services in a post-emergency context. Specifically, the overarching aim of this case was to offer recommendations for how cities can implement a rapid and flexible recovery, thereby seizing the opportunity to implement transformative service redesign. It sought to accomplish this by assessing shifts in city priorities, expectations and public service satisfaction and subsequently proposing improvements to government operations.

The research unfolded in two primary stages:

1. *Assessment of the current context:* In this initial phase, a thorough investigation into the existing conditions was conducted, identifying the needs, capabilities, priorities, and perceived value within urban environments. Desk research and interviews with key stakeholders and users were utilised. This comprehensive exploration served as the foundation for understanding the current service landscape and identifying areas for innovation and redesign.
2. *Development of strategies for service redesign*: The second phase focused on crafting practical suggestions aimed at service redesign. These recommendations emerged from qualitative analyses and insights drawn from focus groups comprised of public administrators and citizens.

By dividing the research into these components, our aim was to not only diagnose the current state of urban services but also propose forward-thinking, actionable strategies for service redesign. This approach positions cities to not just recover from challenges but to evolve their service offerings, making them more responsive, and aligned with the needs and aspirations of their citizens.

This study focuses on a big southern European municipality – a historical capital – heavily struck by the lockdown measures. It is characterised by extraordinary cultural and artistic values and a robust tourism-based sector. Moreover, it released one of the earliest post-pandemic urban strategies. This empirical analysis hinges on the evaluation and evolution of the citizens' expectations of and satisfaction with municipal services before and after the pandemic's two initial waves, spanning from March 2020 to October 2020, coinciding with the commencement of the vaccination campaign in January 2021. Key findings emerged from this research, including a preference among citizens for engaging with government services online, especially when professional assistance is available. Furthermore, increased satisfaction with online services during the pandemic underscores the need for digital readiness and redesign in certain policy areas, such as mobility. Exploring the interplay between expectations, performance, and satisfaction revealed that the citizens most satisfied with a specific public service are those who have their expectations managed effectively and subsequently experience superior service performance. This underscores the importance of clear and transparent communication regarding service expectations. Lastly, the research highlighted the potential benefits of co-design and co-delivery in facilitating a mutual understanding of expectations and organisational feasibility, ultimately streamlining the redesign process.

In the following subsections of this section, we provide an in-depth exploration of the study's background, the methods employed, and the insights derived from our research findings.

3.1 Research Context

Governments aim to enhance public well-being and meet stakeholder expectations through actions such as regulation, service delivery, policy formulation, and public goods provision (Bellé et al., 2023). Historically, most governments have failed to assess the value they create with citizens and involve them in service design (Osborne et al., 2013; Nasi et al., 2024). Additionally governments often struggle to govern the nexus between objectives, needs and outcomes (Knapp, 1984).

The COVID-19 pandemic sparked a debate on the value of government services as local governments grappled with changing citizen expectations and priorities shaped by the new daily routines. To meet such expectations, governments have to comprehend the evolving context in terms of needs, capacity, preferences and value, ensuring consistency with the existing status quo while making necessary adjustments. This process entails recognising and supporting changes in value rather than inventing entirely new solutions.

3.1.1 Assessing Value through Citizen Satisfaction

One way to gauge the value of government services is by evaluating citizen satisfaction. The importance of citizen satisfaction gained prominence in the late 1970s and early 1980s, coinciding with the growth of instruments such as the Service Quality Model SERVQUAL, which was used to measure customer satisfaction in service industries (Bouckaert & Van de Walle, 2003). Several scholars (i.e. Van Ryzin, 2015) explored the relationship between expectations, satisfaction, and overall community judgment, arguing that the quality and outcomes of government services significantly influence citizens' subjective evaluations of their community as a desirable place to live, thereby impacting residence and relocation decisions.

The COVID-19 pandemic reshaped citizens' expectations and behaviours due to the restrictions and new practices it gave rise to. Public services designed to address immediate challenges, such as social distancing and limited physical access, may now no longer suffice. They may also fail to meet the evolved expectations that have arisen in the post-pandemic context (Vargo, 2008). Consequently, understanding how citizens' expectations evolve is crucial for local governments to redesign services, allocate resources, and innovate to meet citizens' needs.

3.1.2 Challenges of Meeting Diverse Needs

Local governments must cater to a diverse population with heterogeneous needs, making one-size-fits-all solutions impractical. Designing services that align with evolving expectations is complex due to the challenge of envisioning end-to-end experiences from multiple stakeholders' perspectives. Service design emerges as an innovative approach to improving the quality of services, programmes, and policies considering expectations, satisfaction, and feasibility (Clarke & Craft, 2018). Service design was traditionally limited to engineering and architecture but has recently expanded into a multidisciplinary field that incorporates insights from psychology, cognitive sciences, and anthropology. It focuses on the user experience of citizens and providers, encourages early experimentation and prototyping to prevent later failures, and prioritises value delivery. In the context of public services, service design involves creating user-centred products, services, solutions, and experiences (Bason & Austin, 2019).

3.1.3 Co-Design and the Creative Process

Service design fosters user participation to create new forms of value through co-design. Service design acknowledges the absence of well-defined problems and embraces divergent thinking to generate multiple ideas, followed by convergent thinking to refine and select the best solution. To this end, qualitative techniques, such as ethnographic research, service journeys, participant observations and prototyping, are used to facilitate user-centred problem-solving. To consolidate the design process and community involvement, a critical appraisal of service design methods is essential.

Thus, this study employs a range of methods to frame its background, assess citizen expectations and satisfaction with public services pre- and post-COVID-19, and deepen the understanding of the human experience of both citizens and providers. These methods and tools inform recommendations for service redesign.

3.2 Methods

We used service design tools to deepen insights into both citizens' and providers' experience with services. In doing so, we gained a better understanding of user expectations, the user journey, and organisational processes. This information allowed us to formulate recommendations to redesign the services that create value for their users.

A research methodology combining focus groups and directed observational studies was selected for its interactive nature. Importantly, the methodology adopted a systemic and holistic view, acknowledging and incorporating complexity, chaos, ambiguity, fuzziness, and dynamic forces rather than simplifying them for analytical ease (Gummesson, 2006). This was particularly relevant for our research, where the complexity and uncertainty were heightened due to the numerous interactions between users and service providers (Sparks, 2001). Therefore, this method was deemed most suitable for the depth and breadth of analysis required in this study.

3.2.1 Understanding the User through the Use of Personas and Focus Groups

Personas were developed from in-depth interviews with eight citizens. The interviews focused on identifying perceived differences in service provision that might influence citizens' experiences. The identified differences resulted from the clustering of the selected data's relevant themes (Miles & Huberman, 1994). The insights derived from the in-depth interviews provided an understanding of the service user's background from a broader real-world perspective. The insights that were derived from the interviews were related to the specific service system to be analysed.

Building on this methodological foundation, we applied Tremblay and colleagues' (Tremblay et al., 2010a) framework for utilising EFGs and CFGs as it presents a robust methodology that has been widely used over the past years for the refinement of artefact design. By adapting EFGs and CFGs within the service design process, organisations can ensure that their services are not only innovative and user-centred but also validated through rigorous user engagement. This approach aligns closely with the principles of user-centred design, emphasising the importance of understanding user needs and validating solutions through iterative development and testing.

The careful distinction between EFGs and CFGs aligns with our approach of embracing complexity and avoids oversimplification. For both types of focus group, a meticulously crafted script was developed, ensuring that each focus group's unique objectives were effectively met and that the insights generated were both relevant and robust.

Two methods were used to recruit participants for the interviews and focus groups. To recruit citizens and entrepreneurs, we used the municipality's Facebook page. We collected information and selected participants who are (i) aged between 18 and 64, (ii) residing in the central area of the municipality, (iii) unemployed, self-employed, or employed and (iv) working in the mobility industry (i.e. taxi drivers, mobility managers, etc.). Each citizen was offered transportation reimbursement for their travel to the focus group site and an Amazon Gift Card of €25 in value. As for public managers for the focus groups, we recruited those who are (i) engaged in delivering the service to citizens, (ii) engaged in mobility services, and (iii) engaged in the management of the Information Technology (IT) services for digital services. No compensation was offered to the recruited public managers.

All the focus groups were conducted in person while respecting the COVID-19 restrictions in place at the time of data collection. Before starting each focus group, the moderators introduced the project, explained the objectives, and provided general information about the focus group. We conducted a total of two Exploratory Focus Groups (EFGs) and one Confirmatory Focus Group (CFG), involving three panels of participants. The first panel included eight citizens, some of whom were entrepreneurs living and investing in the city; the second panel consisted of six public managers. Finally, a confirmatory panel was held, comprising six citizens and six public managers.

The scripts were prepared in advance in Italian to address the key questions of the study, which were designed to deepen our understanding of expectation and satisfaction with services and consequently identify strengths and challenges to address in case of the redesign.

The focus group discussions were audio-recorded and professionally transcribed. The transcripts were analysed using computer-assisted qualitative data analysis software (CAQDAS). We utilised Dedoose version 7.6.17 (www.dedoose.com). In the following, we draw illustrative examples from each transcript (King, 1998): short quotes are used to support specific points of interpretation and longer quotes are used to convey a sense of the original discussions.

3.3 Findings

3.3.1 Understanding Users' Needs and Ideas to Innovate Service Opportunities

The exploratory and confirmatory focus groups conducted with citizens, entrepreneurs, and public managers revealed key shifts in service expectations and user experiences in the post-COVID 19 context. The findings are organised around three pivotal factors influencing the evolving user journey:

(1) a revised schedule of daily routines,
(2) the widespread adoption of smart working practices, and
(3) the customisation of services to address concerns around health, access, and inclusion.

(1) A Revised Schedule of Daily Events: Shifts in Routine and Service Use Patterns

In the first exploratory focus group, conducted with citizens – some of whom were entrepreneurs – participants were asked what factors they consider when deciding where to live. Following individual brainstorming, their answers were categorised into five areas: (i) nature and environment (e.g. climate, open-air spaces for walking or training), (ii) job opportunities, (iii) cultural heritage and offerings, (iv) the area's human scale and social capital, and (v) services (especially health, mobility, and education).

When discussing services, participants focused on quality and accessibility. They expressed a preference for modern, user-friendly channels of interaction that reflect the diverse needs of target users. Examples included digital services accessible to older adults with limited tech skills, booking systems usable by people with visual impairments, and clear information formats for users with cognitive challenges. One participant described what they expect in terms of healthcare quality:

> '*I expect access to professionals with the right competencies and a multidisciplinary vision of a health problem ... I expect professionals to listen to the patients, to their questions and needs.*' (P1)

Another highlighted the importance of evidence-based decision-making in service provision:

> '*Through technology and data management, health professionals should innovate their decisions about diagnosis and therapies. Data is interconnected, and it should be used properly.*' (P3)

A third emphasised usability:

> '*I don't want to queue to pay for services, including healthcare services ... It has to be easy for the user to access a service and go through its delivery process.*' (P2)

In mobility, participants generally appreciated the variety of transport options in the city. However, they identified major usability challenges. One participant commented:

> *'I would always use my bike, but the metro construction sites, traffic, pollution and the lack of adequate bike lanes make it too dangerous to consider it as a main means of transportation.'* (P4)

Another pointed to poor intermodality:

> *'I now want to ride my car everywhere, but it's hard to find a parking spot. I would switch to other means of transportation. Individually they are all good, but interconnectivity among them is still very limited.'* (P5)

Participants noted that all urban transport modes – bikes, motorcycles, buses, taxis, and private cars – use the same roads, creating congestion and infrastructural degradation. The current system, described as a static backbone, lacks the flexibility to adapt to emerging needs.

Public managers confirmed these changes. They highlighted, for instance, that taxi usage had shifted from being dominated by business travellers and tourists (over 50 per cent of rides pre-COVID) to broader citizen use, creating demand for lower prices and changes in peak-hour service patterns. They also noted the limited capacity of public transportation and its rising operational costs due to altered school and business hours and the need to deploy additional transport options, such as converting tourist buses into school buses.

(2) The Widespread Adoption of Smart Working and Its Implications

Participants identified smart working as a major factor shaping both housing needs and expectations of service delivery. While most citizens agreed that the city had improved over time, they voiced concerns about rising inequality. One concern was housing affordability – 'housing may become too expensive for some citizens' – which may lead to exclusion from the city.

Another participant linked housing conditions to the inadequacy of home spaces for new work and life routines: 'A two-bedroom apartment for a family of four to five people did not offer adequate space for studying and working.'

This highlighted the impact of smart working and lockdowns, which forced many families to adapt to confined and ill-equipped domestic environments. Public managers similarly acknowledged that citizens' routines had changed. One noted:

> '*COVID has taught us the importance of capillarity of services. Once the first wave of COVID-19 hit the city, we had to close down all the offices but the central one. Fortunately, most register's office services were digitised, but some target groups were not capable of accessing online services, and we cannot afford to leave anyone behind.*' (PM1)

They observed that even young citizens may be digitally excluded if living in poverty:

> '*Even a young citizen with a critical poverty situation is not able to access online services.*' (PM2)

Participants also suggested flexible service models adapted to these changing routines. Ideas included dynamic bus sizes for peak and off-peak hours, intelligent traffic systems to manage flow, and integrated solutions enabling seamless inter-mobility across local, regional, and national services.

(3) Customisation of Services to Address Concerns around Health, Access, and Inclusion

Participants stressed the importance of services that are responsive to real, complex user conditions, especially in digital service delivery. They generally praised the city's online mobility parking pass system for its clarity and ease of use for 'standard' users, that is, municipal residents with privately owned vehicles. However, frustrations emerged when dealing with non-traditional use cases.

One such case, explored in the Confirmatory Focus Group, involved a resident using a car registered to a nonresident family member. Others involved leased cars or company-owned vehicles. These situations exposed limitations in the design logic of the digital service, which was built on the assumption that service users are residents who own their cars.

This misalignment led to reduced satisfaction and increased friction. The issue was further compounded by the absence of coordinated databases linking residency, ownership, and license plate registration. As one participant summarised:

> '*The service works well for those who fit the model, but if you fall outside of that – even just a bit – it becomes frustrating.*' (P3)

During the CFG, citizens expressed a clear willingness to engage in co-design and problem-solving. In contrast, public managers often relied on bureaucratic jargon to explain design constraints and showed limited openness to innovation. Some justified the status quo by referencing institutional and organisational limitations. Nevertheless, the feedback from both exploratory and confirmatory sessions led the municipality to improve the parking pass service. Adjustments were made to address the residency–ownership–plate mismatch and to extend service accessibility in line with users' lived realities and the organisational capacity of the city.

3.4 Discussion and Conclusions

This study explored the application of service design methods to understand citizens' evolving expectations and experiences with municipal services in the post-COVID-19 context. Through exploratory and confirmatory focus groups involving citizens, entrepreneurs, and public managers, we identified key tensions between lived realities and institutional logics, particularly in the domain of urban mobility services.

Three pivotal factors emerged as shaping the post-pandemic user journey:

(1) a revised schedule of daily events,
(2) the widespread adoption of smart working practices, and
(3) a growing need for customisation and inclusivity in public services.

These factors were reflected in concrete experiences and expectations across stakeholder groups. The findings in Subsection 3.3 illustrate how these shifts challenge conventional assumptions in service design – particularly around eligibility, accessibility, and infrastructure – and reveal the need for adaptive, user-informed innovation.

3.4.1 Observation 1: The Impact of COVID-19 on Citizens' Needs, Expectations and Satisfaction with Public Services, Emphasising Digitalisation

The COVID-19 pandemic has significantly reshaped citizens' needs, expectations, and satisfaction levels regarding public services. Notably, a prevailing preference for digital services has emerged among the majority of citizens. This paradigm shift necessitates the implementation of innovative strategies leveraging the transformative potential of technology by local governments (Micacchi et al., 2025).

Rather than attempting to address every conceivable challenge, local governments can channel their efforts into fostering innovation. This entails strengthening urban systems' capacity to tackle a diverse array of issues and generate various public values (Meijer & Bolivar, 2016, p. 393). Digitalisation transcends mere technology integration; it encompasses multi-stakeholder involvement, including citizens; the promotion of transparent decision-making processes and the enhancement of public service quality (Gil-Garcia et al., 2014).

To effectively navigate the digital transformation challenge, governments should focus on enhancing their innovative capabilities through the following measures:

- *Cultivating a culture of innovation:* Our exploratory focus group with public managers, as well as the confirmatory group, underscored the presence of cultural resistance within organisations. Siloed structures hinder data sharing and collaboration across departments, impeding the creation of essential invisible infrastructures encompassing data, codes, and repositories.
- *Advancing digital e-leadership*: Recognising that citizens increasingly prefer digitally delivered services, governments must not only adopt new technologies but also embrace novel modes of organisational governance and service delivery (Osborne et al. 2022). Public managers and policymakers must acknowledge the pivotal role of digital transformation and the opportunities it presents.
- *Strengthening communication to leverage expectations*: Transparent communication serves as a vital tool for harnessing citizen expectations and fostering co-production, ultimately enhancing the efficacy of public services.

In light of these imperatives, local governments are poised to navigate the dynamic landscape of digitalisation and meet the evolving needs and expectations of their constituents.

3.4.2 Observation 2: The Interplay between Expectations, Benchmarking and Performance in Service Design

Our investigation revealed a significant interconnection between citizens' expectations, benchmarking, and their assessment of service performance. Our findings underscore the vital importance of considering citizens' needs and expectations from the service design phase (Porumbescu et al., 2021). Relative satisfaction is intricately linked to the perceived quality and performance of services. Employing service design methodologies can facilitate the systematic assessment of citizens' expectations and needs, thereby enabling the delivery of services that align effectively with the preferences and requirements of the targeted user base. Such an approach is pivotal for enhancing the overall quality and relevance of public services within a service design framework.

Observation 3. Co-design and Co-Creation of Services May Foster a Fast Alignment of Objectives-Needs-Outcomes for Services

Satisfaction with services depends upon the user's experience. As such, since value is not created until the user integrates and applies the municipality's resources to other resources in their own context, it is not possible to design innovation and services as pre-defined outputs (Vargo, 2008). In our study, the municipality designed an efficient process for delivering its mobility parking pass, taking into account resources and barriers (such as the dependency on input data from the Department of Motor Vehicles). However, the municipality failed to *take into account the users' actual needs and the users' journey*. The service was designed under the assumption that citizens are residents of the Municipality and they own a car registered under their names; the reality is different. The service was based on the assumption that all users are municipal residents who own and drive vehicles registered in their own names; however, this does not reflect the actual diversity of user situations. Several people do not formally reside in the Municipality; thus, they live there, and a large portion of the population have decided to lease a car, or are given one from their company.

Consequently, a necessary condition to set the right goals for service design is understanding the overall needs that a service must meet (Nasi et al., 2023). However, more is needed as it does not provide qualitative attributes to identify the processes and peripheral elements that create value for citizens.

Service design may represent a possible methodology to assist in a city's transformation as it offers the opportunity to assess the users' needs and their journey and to design possible solutions that meet the feasibility and organisational capacity of the local governments as it creates new kinds of value between actors within a socio-material configuration (Kimbell, 2011). From our study, we learnt that co-design is not simply a process of user empowerment but rather one of balancing and synthesising user needs and expectations with the professional expertise of care staff and the inevitable resource constraints of public service delivery. A key challenge for the facilitation of such co-design is *the balance between innovation and reality*. On the one hand, it is essential to keep the early stages of the co-design process as open as possible in order to explore user needs in the most holistic manner. On the other hand, resource constraints inevitably have to be acknowledged when turning expressed needs into service offerings and triangulating how citizens' expectations of and experiences with public services evolved after the COVID-19 pandemic. Citizens expect digital public services, and they are willing to collaborate to find adequate solutions that meet their relative expectations. Governments also have a good understanding of the evolution of needs and expectations; however, they may not be adequately equipped to cope with the degree of transformation required to adapt to citizen's new expectations. For these reasons, governments should invest in their innovation capacity and enhance their toolkits to frame needs and expectations by identifying key stakeholders and engaging with them. A one-size-fits-all service often fails to reflect the realities of a diverse population. In this context, a stakeholder map is particularly useful as it enables public managers to systematically identify all relevant actors – both users and institutional counterparts – and to categorise them based on their influence, interests, and experiences with the service. By doing so, governments can prioritise engagement with critical user groups, uncover differentiated expectations, and tailor service design accordingly. A stakeholder map also supports a more nuanced understanding of the user journey, revealing points of friction, satisfaction, and exclusion across different segments. This makes it an essential tool for designing inclusive, targeted interventions. The broader challenge in service redesign is to empower both users and public managers in a way that balances expectations, institutional capacity, and available resources. To do so, public managers must involve citizens from the earliest stages of problem framing and develop capabilities to assess both evolving needs and the responsiveness of services to those needs.

4 Embracing Citizen-Strategic Orientation in Public Service Design: The Application of the Double Diamond Design Process to Value Creation

In this section, we venture into the realm of PSL, which revolutionises our understanding of public services by viewing them through the lens of 'services'. This perspective unlocks a deeper appreciation of the dynamics inherent in public service delivery. Rooted in the ideas of Osborne (2018), PSL emphasises the pivotal role of 'participation' and 'value'. Participation here is not just passive but involves citizens actively contributing to public service redesign. The concept of value under PSL goes beyond mere delivery; it is realised and enriched when citizens actively use and experience the services.

Under the PSL framework, citizen engagement is not a mere formality but a fundamental aspect of the nature of public service. This implies a transformative approach where citizens' experiences, through continuous participation, shape the creation, planning, and design of public services (Nasi & Choi, 2023). Such an approach enables PSOs to align more closely with citizens' expectations and needs (Bovaird & Loeffler, 2012). Public service organisations with a citizen-strategic orientation foster an organisational culture attuned to understanding and integrating user-defined value, thereby enhancing sustainable public service delivery (Osborne et al., 2021). However, the involvement of citizens in the decision-making process often remains superficial (Rose et al., 2018), with PSOs hesitating to fully embrace citizen participation in goal setting and service provision.

This section also addresses the challenges of citizen engagement, such as collaborative governance, stakeholder relationship management and the effectiveness of engagement strategies (Voorberg et al., 2015; Osborne et al., 2016; Nabatchi et al., 2017). In response, service design theory emerges as a potential game-changer, championing empathy and stakeholder involvement to foster a culture of citizen-strategic orientation. Service design's strength lies in its empathetic approach, engaging users and stakeholders to comprehensively understand problems and contexts, thereby driving creative and feasible solutions (Reason et al., 2015).

In this section, we posit that service design methods and tools are instrumental in fostering a citizen-strategic orientation. By blurring traditional engagement barriers, these strategies prioritise empathising with service users to frame problems and solutions that create meaningful value. In the following subsections, we present a mixed-method analysis focusing on local governments, starting with a survey to identify a public service area with notable citizen dissatisfaction. A subsequent qualitative analysis, guided by design strategies, delves into these issues to devise citizen-centred solutions that are organisationally viable.

This section suggests that design strategies are not only effective but essential in advancing citizen-centric service orientation. Service design practices, particularly *co-design*, bring together diverse actors, fostering an environment where collective reflections on experiences catalyse innovative co-creation opportunities (Akama & Prendiville, 2013; Vink et al., 2021b).

The following subsections of this section explore the theoretical framework, describe our methodology, present our findings, and discuss the broader implications and potential directions for future research in this field.

4.1 Background

Public service organisations face the formidable task of catering to the diverse and often heterogeneous needs of large populations. The complexity of these needs defies the simplicity of 'one-size-fits-all' solutions. Furthermore, the value that an individual ascribes to a service is intrinsically linked to their unique personal needs, values, expectations, and experiences – factors over which PSOs have limited direct influence.

4.1.1 The Role of Co-Creation in Value Creation

Research on co-creation highlights that the potential value of a service is determined not only by a PSO's understanding of citizens' value creation processes but also by the citizens' own experiences (Patricio et al., 2011). Therefore, actively involving citizens in the entire service process – from exploration and creation to reflection and implementation and from commissioning and design to delivery and evaluation – becomes pivotal. Such involvement is essential for understanding local needs, aspirations and resources, thereby informing critical decisions about enhancing community well-being and choosing effective solutions (Trischler et al., 2018).

4.1.2 Co-Commissioning and Co-Design: Leveraging Citizen Expertise

Co-commissioning and co-design activities integrate user experiences into the planning of public services. These approaches capitalise on citizens' expertise, promoting the co-creation of value in both future and present contexts (Nabatchi et al., 2017). While initial PSL research concentrated on service co-production and citizen contributions to contemporary public service challenges (Voorber et al., 2015; Osborne et al., 2016), there is a burgeoning interest in exploring how citizen participation in commissioning and design can generate ideas and solutions that elevate user value (Vargo et al., 2008; Gronroos & Voima, 2013).

Beyond Traditional Participation: Co-Design for Future Use

Co-commissioning and co-design go beyond traditional forms of citizen participation. They focus on envisioning future use scenarios, offering insights into citizens' experiences and needs for a more refined citizen orientation (Steen et al., 2011; Wetter-Edman et al., 2014). As mentioned in Section 2, co-design is seen as a collaborative means to address complex societal challenges, particularly in the ideation stage of the public sector service design process (Trischler et al., 2019). Through design tools, citizens and professionals engage in a reciprocal exchange of service experiences, collaboratively defining service value (Sanders & Dandavate, 1999) and navigating the complexities of tacit, hard-to-transfer information (Von Hippel, 1994).

Current Research and the Promise of Service Design

As already explored in Sections 1 and 2, contemporary research in public service design primarily focuses on engaging with users and incorporating their experiences into decision-making processes (Trischler et al., 2019; Trischler & Trischler, 2020). In addressing this engagement challenge, service design emerges as a transformative approach that emphasises empathy, fostering a profound understanding of problems and their context by involving users and stakeholders. By articulating questions that drive engagement, service design facilitates the generation of innovative, consensus-driven solutions. These solutions undergo testing for feasibility, with prototypes iteratively refined for broader implementation.

This study aims to deepen the understanding of how citizen involvement in co-design practices influences the design process and outcomes within PSOs. We explored how this participatory approach impacts the framing of problems and the generation of innovative service ideas and solutions. The next subsection outlines our mixed-method approach, which integrated quantitative and qualitative methods to investigate the strategic orientation of citizens in public service design.

4.2 Methods

In this section, we investigate how service design tools can be utilised to engage citizens in public service design and delivery. Anchoring our approach to service design theory, we focused on the active and collaborative involvement of users, positioning them as 'experts of their experience' in addressing complex societal issues (Sanders & Stappers, 2008). This approach leverages the collective creativity of diverse team members (Steen, 2013) and aims to enhance the capacity of a local government in framing and solving service-related problems. We adopted a mixed-methods strategy, encompassing both quantitative and qualitative sequential studies.

Our sequential study design unfolded in two interactive phases: the collection and analysis of quantitative data to establish the initial scope and qualitative data analysis for an in-depth exploration of the findings (Ivankova et al., 2006; Teddlie &Tashakkori, 2006; Stentz et al., 2012). This dual approach allowed for a comprehensive understanding of the research problem, leveraging the strengths of both methods while addressing their individual limitations (Creswell & Clark, 2007; Mele & Belardinelli, 2019).

We adopted the Design Council's Double Diamond design process (2007), which includes four distinct phases, namely (i) Discover, (ii) Define, (iii) Develop, and (iv) Deliver (see Section 2 for more details on this methodology). To tailor the Double Diamond process to our specific needs, we implemented the following modified approach.

Discover and Define (Phases 1 and 2): For the Discover phase, which involves a comprehensive approach to understanding the problem at hand and includes gathering extensive information to immerse oneself in the experiences and perspectives of those impacted by the issue, thereby gaining deep insights and avoiding assumptions, we developed a quantitative observational survey to retrospectively examine user experiences with public services, focusing on identifying gaps in the value they provide. This involved categorising the public services offered by the municipality into key types, such as institutional services (e.g. local taxation), services to individuals (e.g. education), and territorial services (e.g. maintenance and waste management). These services were available through multiple channels, including in-person and online.

We then conducted a quantitative analysis to evaluate the discrepancies in perceived importance and satisfaction across these services, asking citizens to rate each on a seven-point Likert scale, where 1 indicated the lowest level of importance or satisfaction and 7 indicated the highest.

Utilising the insights gained from the survey, we focused on *defining the problem more clearly*. We selected one public service that exhibited a significant gap in importance versus satisfaction. Our goal was to deepen our understanding of the underlying issues, priorities, and user preferences through qualitative design strategies. We selected this service to explore in greater depth, using qualitative design strategies to examine user experiences, expectations, and pain points. Through this process, we developed a well-defined problem statement: 'How might we redesign the service to accommodate diverse user scenarios while ensuring ease of access, fairness, and administrative feasibility?' This problem framing captured both the technical and experiential dimensions of the challenge and provided a concrete foundation for guiding subsequent co-design and solution development efforts.

To further explore the identified service gaps, we organised focus groups comprising both citizens and service professionals. These sessions were instrumental in uncovering real-world challenges as perceived by users.

Develop and Deliver (Phases 3 and 4): In the third phase of the Double Diamond process, which emphasises the development of solutions, our approach was to further refine and expand upon the insights gained in the earlier phases.

To support the development of innovative service ideas, we organised additional focus groups. In line with standard methodological practice, each individual focus group was composed of relatively homogeneous participants – such as citizens, entrepreneurs, or public managers – to create a safe and comfortable environment for discussion, reduce potential conflict, and facilitate the open exchange of ideas within shared experiential contexts. This structure also allowed us to clearly capture distinct stakeholder perspectives. Multiple focus groups were then employed to ensure diversity across the broader dataset and to capture the range of perspectives necessary for comprehensive service design.

These sessions were specifically designed to foster creative thinking and collaborative problem-solving, focusing on the generation of innovative service ideas that could significantly improve overall value. This collaborative environment was crucial for brainstorming sessions, enabling participants to build on each other's ideas and leading to the development of potentially transformative solutions. The objective of these sessions was to leverage the collective intelligence and creativity of the group to explore a wide array of service innovations. These could range from incremental improvements to existing services to groundbreaking new offerings that could redefine user experiences.

By facilitating these discussions in a structured, yet open-ended, manner, we aimed to uncover unique insights and ideas that could be further developed and tested in subsequent phases of the model.

This step was instrumental in transitioning from understanding and defining the problem space to actively creating and shaping potential solutions. The focus groups served as a dynamic platform for synthesising the gathered knowledge and translating it into actionable service design concepts that could enhance value for users and stakeholders alike. Furthermore, in the last phase, we aimed to validate the feasibility and alignment of the proposed solutions with both citizens' values and the organisation's capabilities. Methodologically, this phase employed user testing, prototype development and iterative design methods. Solutions were evaluated based on their feasibility, effectiveness, and potential impact, leading to the finalisation of the most viable solution for implementation. We employed a method known as 'organisational impact analysis', a service design technique for assessing an organisation's capacity to deliver new services. This approach links the designed user experiences with the organisation's structure and capabilities (Reason et al., 2015). A final focus group with service professionals was conducted to review the proposed service ideas and solutions and select those that both created value and aligned with the organisation's operational capacities.

4.2.1 Data Collection: A Mixed-Methods Approach in a European Municipality

Our empirical analysis was conducted in a local southern European government in a developed European region serving over 170,000 residents, including a significant proportion of recent immigrants. The municipality spans four zones and a city centre. The survey explored citizens' perceptions of importance and satisfaction regarding *eleven local public services*. These services spanned three main areas: services for citizens, services for the territory, and institutional services. The participants in the survey were 500, a number representative of the city's diverse population of 170,000 across its four zones. The participants were selected based on gender, age (18 years and above) and geographical area of residence.

The distribution of the survey took place in various municipal facilities such as the main library, the registry office's welcoming area, and the municipality's primary one-stop-service information office.

Respondents were approached at these locations and invited to participate on a voluntary basis. To ensure a representative sample, participants were screened using a few demographic questions (gender, age, and geographical area of residence) before proceeding to complete the survey. This process allowed us to achieve a balanced demographic representation, ensuring the robustness and validity of the findings.

The survey questions focused on (i) participants' usage of the services, (ii) the perceived importance of each service, (iii) the importance of specific service attributes in determining satisfaction, (iv) overall satisfaction with the services, and (v) satisfaction with particular dimensions of the services.

Among the services investigated, education services had the most significant gap in terms of importance/satisfaction; therefore, we decided to focus on education services. To further explore the identified service gaps, we organised a total of three focus groups. Participants representing the city's diverse demographic spread were selected through a municipality-issued call for interest across local schools.

The first focus group comprised eight parents with children in various education services; they volunteered in response to school-distributed invitations. The second focus group included twelve professionals crucial to the design and delivery of educational services. These individuals ranged from the deputy mayors overseeing education and digital innovation to senior managers, school principals, and teachers from schools randomly selected across the city's zones.

Following this part of the Develop phase, another focus group was organised with the key figures in local educational policy and strategy, who had also contributed to the previous focus groups. Each focus group session spanned approximately three hours.

Prepared scripts steered the discussions towards crucial aspects of the study, notably, understanding citizens' expectations and satisfaction to identify users' needs, service challenges, and areas ripe for redesign.

The discussions were audio-recorded and transcribed professionally. Using CAQDAS and framework analysis methods, we meticulously processed the transcripts. Initial manual analysis allowed us to familiarise ourselves with the content, develop a coding structure, and identify emerging themes and patterns. Iterative analysis of these themes led to a comprehensive understanding of the key points raised during the discussions.

To ensure inter-coder reliability, multiple researchers independently coded a subset of transcripts and compared results, resolving discrepancies through discussion to reach consensus on final codes and categories. Iterative analysis of these themes led to a comprehensive understanding of the key points raised during the discussions.

Our findings highlight major themes with illustrative examples, succinct quotes for specific interpretations and longer excerpts to capture the essence of the discussions. This qualitative analysis not only enhances our understanding of public sentiments regarding education services but also informs improvements in service design.

4.3 Findings

4.3.1 Discover and Define Phases: Uncovering Needs and Gaps in Public Education Services

The observational survey focused on enhancing our understanding of how citizens perceive the importance and satisfaction associated with eleven local public services. These services were categorised into three groups: citizen-oriented services such as social and health care, education, libraries and mobility services; territorial services including water quality, environmental, and city works; and local police and institutional services such as local tax administration.

The results revealed a clear preference among citizens for services that directly affect them, with education services showing the most significant gap between their perceived importance and satisfaction. This finding underscores the critical need for improvement in education services to align with citizen expectations.

We then focused more in depth on *education services*. This decision was driven by the insights gathered from our quantitative analysis, which indicated significant issues within these services. Additionally, literature on public service design underscores that in areas such as education, PSOs primarily provide a service offering without directly creating value for the users. The real value in such services emerges from how the users (in this case, students) interact with and utilise these offerings in their own lives. Osborne (2018) articulated this concept effectively, using the example of a teacher delivering a mathematics lecture. While the teacher provides the educational content, the lecture's true value is realised when the student engages with the material in a manner that enriches their knowledge and life experience.

Therefore, education services present a unique opportunity to explore and enhance value creation from the users' perspective. An in-depth analysis of such services allows us to delve into how service offerings can be optimised to better align with and enrich the user's personal and educational journey.

Focus Groups with Service Professionals

For our qualitative analysis of education services, a focus group comprising service professionals (SP) was convened to examine the *nature and user experience of these services*. The discussions revealed that the design and execution of services such as admissions, payments, and educational processes predominantly follow an *inside-out* approach. This approach, as highlighted by one participant (SP1) from the education department, tends to prioritise internal coordination and adherence to timelines, often at the expense of usability, accessibility, and cross-service synergies. The participant noted, 'The service process is organised to fulfil the timelines of each office involved; it is the sum of activities designed without considering the ownership of coordination and the users' expectations' (SP1).

A recurring theme in the discussion was the critical importance of fostering a trust-based relationship with parents, which could be achieved through enhanced communication strategies and specific operational actions. One participant (SP3), for example, underscored the need for clarity in the admission criteria, advising that the education department should transparently communicate how points are allocated for admission lists to guide parents better.

Further, the participants acknowledged the necessity of organisational innovation and the simplification of service processes. One participant (SP2) 2, in particular, pointed out the growing diversity in the demographic and ethnic backgrounds of parents, emphasising the need for inclusive communication strategies. The professional stressed, 'Not all parents speak Italian; all our communications should reflect the background of our stakeholders, to be inclusive' (SP2).

In summary, the focus groups with education service professionals provided valuable insights into their perspectives as internal service users, as well as their understanding of external service users' expectations and experiences. The professionals identified two key strategies for enhancing the educational benefits for users and maintaining a trust-based relationship with citizens: streamlining processes and ensuring transparent communication between all stakeholders.

Focus Group with Parents

In the focus group with parents (P), the participants emphasised the importance of a trust-based relationship with education professionals, particularly those involved in daily school activities. They advocated for greater parent and family engagement in the service design process and stressed the need for effective, ongoing communication to strengthen trust.

The participants pinpointed two specific areas within the education system that could benefit from improvements to bolster parent-school trust: the *transparency of enrolment lists* and the *enhancement of communication* about children's daily activities at school. Parent 7 (P7), expressing a desire for immediate transparency during the online admission process, said, 'I would expect to know how much we score right when I fill in the online admission request for my kid.

As criteria are known, this signals a transparent process' (P7) At the time of the study, the online system did not instantly reveal the score for each application, making the process less transparent.

Communication was another major area of concern. Despite the schools providing detailed, handwritten diaries complete with pictures and descriptions, parents found these insufficient. For example, Parent 3 lamented, 'We often miss all details about our kids' school days, as my mother-in-law or the nanny pick them up and they don't report back what activities the children got engaged in ...' (P3). Similarly, Parent 4 pointed out, 'The school invests a lot of the teachers' time in handwriting a diary that nobody reads' (P4). These comments underscored a gap in the effectiveness of current communication methods, suggesting an opportunity for digital solutions such as educational apps for teacher–parent communication.

Develop and Deliver Phases: How to Redesign Education Services

Armed with the insights from the quantitative analysis and focus groups, we developed a script to engage key educational professionals in discussing the most pertinent issues and the feasibility of the proposed solutions in the Develop phase. The subsequent focus group reviewed this material, focusing on solutions to communication challenges that could enhance the trust-based relationship between teachers and parents.

The participants discussed both immediate solutions, such as daily digital reports to parents, and long-term strategies, such as streamlining the enrolment process with organisational and technological modifications. During discussions about transitioning from written diaries to a digital app for teacher–parent communication, the group considered the deviation from the municipality's educational culture and policy. Participant 1 from the programming department highlighted the city's commitment to human interaction and the value placed on teachers' efforts in creating daily diaries. Moreover, the participant discussed the city's existing digital communication channel, suggesting its underutilisation and the potential to enhance its use, given the resources already invested in it. This channel facilitates both one-way institutional communications from schools to parents and two-way personal interactions, thus offering a blend of traditional and digital methods.

In summary, the focus groups' discussions aimed to reconcile varying stakeholder perspectives and find a balanced approach to service redesign that aligns with the municipality's cultural values and technological capabilities.

4.4 Discussion and Conclusion

4.4.1 Enhancing Public Services through Citizen Engagement and Co-Design

This section explored the potential of service design practices to cultivate a citizen-strategic orientation in public service innovation. Drawing on both quantitative and qualitative data, we examined how citizens' expectations, experiences, and priorities can inform service strategy within a local government context, with a specific focus on public education services.

Our findings reinforce the idea that understanding citizens' perceptions of importance and satisfaction can complement traditional problem-framing methods in public service organisations (PSOs), enabling a more context-sensitive and value-oriented approach. In particular, the identification of education services as an area marked by high importance but low satisfaction provided a clear rationale for deeper investigation using design tools. The quantitative analysis highlighted education as the service with the largest satisfaction gap, indicating both strategic importance and opportunity for value creation. The qualitative findings from focus groups with service professionals and parents offered crucial insights into the specific service elements shaping that gap, especially in terms of transparency, communication, inclusivity, and user engagement.

4.4.2 Observation 1: Reorientation towards a User-Strategic Approach

Findings from the focus groups reveal a misalignment between internal service priorities and the lived experiences of users. For example, while service professionals described the admissions and payment processes as efficient from an administrative standpoint, parents emphasised their lack of transparency and the difficulty of navigating them without timely, clear communication. The request by one parent to receive real-time scoring during the online admissions process (P7) directly illustrates this disconnect.

This reinforces the need for PSOs to *reorient strategy around user experience*, moving beyond an internal logic of coordination to embrace a more participatory, co-designed approach. Involving users – regardless of citizenship or residency status – in early stages of problem framing allows PSOs to generate more responsive, inclusive, and legitimate service solutions. In education services, this would mean co-designing with parents not only at the point of delivery but also during the planning and policy formulation stages.

4.4.3 Observation 2: Addressing Challenges in Service Development

Although participants – including service professionals – recognised the value of innovation and inclusivity (e.g. through multilingual communication strategies as SP2 noted), they also expressed concern about institutional and cultural constraints. For instance, the idea of replacing handwritten diaries with a digital app was met with hesitation due to the municipality's cultural emphasis on human interaction and the symbolic value placed on teachers' manual efforts. This reflects broader tensions between innovation and institutional norms, where even seemingly minor changes must be reconciled with policy values and existing workflows.

This underscores the importance of a structured, stepwise approach to service development, one that combines user-centred innovation with an assessment of organisational feasibility. Service design tools can support this balance by making visible where innovation aligns – or conflicts – with resource constraints, legacy systems, and cultural values.

Both parents and service professionals converged on the importance of trust-based relationships in public education services. However, they articulated this through different lenses: parents sought real-time transparency and meaningful updates about their children's experience (P3, P4), while professionals viewed trust as a function of procedural clarity and inclusiveness (SP1, SP3). This divergence illustrates the importance of reconciling multiple stakeholder perspectives through co-design, a process that helps uncover and bridge differences in what constitutes 'value' in public service delivery.

The design-based inquiry also surfaced opportunities to reuse existing assets – such as the municipality's underutilised digital platform – which could be enhanced to meet parental expectations without compromising the cultural commitments to human interaction.

This section demonstrates that citizen engagement and co-design are not supplementary to public service strategy – they are central to its relevance and legitimacy. In education services, value is co-created through relationships, communication, and clarity. By applying design methods, local governments can better frame and respond to the diversity of user needs, translating abstract expectations into actionable improvements.

Further research should explore how co-design processes evolve over time and under different institutional conditions. Integrating both citizen and internal stakeholder voices remains critical to designing services that are not only innovative but also implementable and context-sensitive. In doing so, we contribute to both the theoretical development of public service logic and the practical advancement of inclusive, citizen-centred service transformation.

5 Engagement of Vulnerable Groups in Healthcare: Designing a Mobile Health Application to Promote Well-Being

In this section, we explore the pivotal role of mobile health technologies (mHealth) in the realm of service design, with a special focus on optimising healthcare provision for vulnerable groups of patients, particularly patients with lung cancer. Our objective is to contribute to state-of-the-art service design by applying a user-centred approach and harnessing the potential of technology. Notably, our endeavour was driven by a pressing challenge: the dearth of research concerning stakeholders' perceptions of mHealth applications designed for chronic conditions (Dexheimer & Borycki, 2015). Recognising this gap in the existing literature, we viewed it as an opportunity to develop an IT intervention that aligns with the expectations and needs of both clinicians and patients, ultimately aiming to enhance outcomes and reduce healthcare expenditure.

To address this challenge effectively, we adopted a conventional IT design approach, drawing insights from IT design principles, requirement acquisition methodologies, software development practices, medical informatics, and cancer care. This amalgamation of knowledge and expertise led to the creation of LuCApp (Lung Cancer Application), an mHealth app tailored for the management of lung cancer treatment. During the iterative testing phases of LuCApp, new team members joined, and advisory clinicians provided valuable input, emphasising the ongoing commitment to collaborative research and service improvement.

However, as our journey unfolded, a critical deficiency in our standard design approach became apparent: the underrepresentation of the patient's perspective. This shortcoming is particularly significant in the context of chronic disease management, where the collaboration between patients and clinicians is paramount (Holman & Lorig, 2000). In service-oriented fields such as healthcare, customers (in this case, patients) play a pivotal role in co-creating value (Vargo & Akaka, 2012). Therefore, in the subsequent phase of our research, we undertook the recruitment and facilitation of focus groups with patients, shedding light on the transformative potential of technology in enabling patients and clinicians to co-create value in unexpected and profound ways. This experience underscored the importance of intentionally including challenging-to-serve clients, such as severely ill patients, in the IT development process.

Our findings give rise to fundamental questions regarding how we measure service quality and identify the role of the customer in service operations. We confirmed that patients actively participate in value co-creation through their use of the mHealth app to enhance healthcare management. This revelation aligns with previous research emphasising the positive impact of co-creation on perceived value for customers (Auh et al., 2007; Vargo & Lusch, 2008). Moreover, patients and healthcare providers engage in a spectrum of value-creation activities that contribute to improved healthcare and overall quality of life (McColl-Kennedy et al., 2012; Sweeney et al., 2015). Shared decision-making, a form of customer participation, has been shown to lead to improved psychological well-being, enhanced medical status, and greater satisfaction with healthcare providers (McColl-Kennedy et al., 2012; Légaré & Witteman, 2013).

Through our research and intensive engagement, we gained deeper insights into how the user experience, whether from the perspective of clinicians or patients, would evolve through use of the app. This involvement allowed us to amplify the voices of various stakeholders and uncover potential discrepancies between patients' and clinicians' viewpoints. While clinicians initially assumed a comprehensive understanding of patients' needs, behaviours, and expectations, our interactions with patients with lung cancer revealed unforeseen insights. These insights have the potential to inform the design of a technology-enabled care pathway, a concept we elaborate on later in this section. This collaborative effort enabled us to capture emergent knowledge stemming from the interactions between our research team, healthcare practitioners, and patients. The result is a significant contribution to intervention research within the field of operations management, particularly within the intricate context of healthcare (Collins & Browning, 2019).

5.1 Background

This section delves into the relevance of focusing on vulnerable groups such as patients with lung cancer. Lung cancer imposes a substantial burden, exceeding the combined mortality rates of breast, colon, and prostate cancers (World Cancer Research Fund/American Institute for Cancer Research, 2017).

Worryingly, the five-year survival rate for lung cancer remains among the lowest of all major cancers. According to the American Cancer Society, the overall five-year relative survival rate for lung cancer is approximately 27 per cent, significantly lower than that for colon (64 per cent), breast (91 per cent), and prostate (97 per cent) cancers (American Cancer Society, 2024). Tragically, more than half of individuals diagnosed with lung cancer die within one year of diagnosis (National Cancer Institute, 2023).

On a more positive note, advances in screening, diagnostics, and treatment have led to meaningful improvements. The American Lung Association reports that the national five-year survival rate increased by 22 per cent over five years, from 21.7 per cent in 2015 to 26.6 per cent in 2019 (American Lung Association, 2023). Furthermore, global initiatives such as the Lung Ambition

Alliance aim to double the five-year survival rate for lung cancer by 2025, through investments in early detection, targeted therapies, and integrated care models (Meng et al., 2024).

However, this improved survival rate presents the challenge of increased healthcare costs; even after completing active cancer treatments such as surgery, chemotherapy, or radiotherapy, patients continue to grapple with persistent physical and psychological symptoms, necessitating ongoing specialised care (Mayer et al., 2014; Miller et al., 2016). While these patients may enjoy extended lives, they also contribute to the caregiving burden, resulting in higher hospitalisation rates, more frequent emergency room visits, and the increased adoption of palliative treatments. These heightened healthcare demands translate into increased costs for healthcare systems, patients, and caregivers, potentially compromising the patients' overall quality of life.

5.1.1 mHealth to Improve Care Coordination

Addressing interventions to enhance patient self-care and healthcare provider relationships is increasingly vital in chronic diseases such as cancer (Martin et al., 2012). Research highlights that successful care models that improve outcomes and reduce costs focus on bolstering patient and family engagement in self-care while facilitating care coordination and communication among patients and providers (McCarthy et al., 2015), and during the pandemic, there was an unprecedented increase in the adoption of digital health technologies (Fagherazzi et al., 2020; Petracca et al., 2020). Driven by social distancing mandates and the postponement of elective procedures, healthcare providers quickly turned to digital platforms to offer virtual consultations, remote visits, and monitoring (Mahmood et al., 2020). Consequently, healthcare delivery has shifted, with digital platforms enabling care to be brought directly to patients' homes, reducing the need for them to travel to physical healthcare facilities.

This section centres on mobile phones, one of the most accessible forms of IT, also responsible for substantial innovations affecting various aspects of society. Smartphones offer an efficient platform for implementing a wide range of healthcare interventions, from disseminating healthcare information (e.g. via short messages or reminders) to personalised healthcare management (e.g. remote monitoring; Déglise et al., 2012; LoPresti et al., 2015).

mHealth falls under the umbrella of eHealth and encompasses health services and information delivered through mobile technologies such as phones, tablets, and personal digital assistants (PDAs) (World Health Organization, 2016). Numerous studies (Chen et al., 2012; LoPresti et al., 2015) demonstrate that mHealth enhances monitoring, tracking and communication, particularly for patients with chronic conditions. It also has the potential to improve patient satisfaction by expediting the diagnosis and treatment of acute conditions. Remote monitoring through mHealth allows the elderly and patients to remain at home, fostering collaboration and information sharing with clinicians who can stay informed about their conditions (Strandbygaard et al., 2010; Gustafson et al., 2015). The prompt detection and treatment of severe symptoms are facilitated by mHealth, thus reducing complications and preventing readmissions (Jensen et al., 2016). This leads to reduced hospital service utilisation, more efficient use of clinicians' time and enhanced healthcare provider performance (Hill-Kayser et al., 2009). Overall, mHealth can transition from a focus on cure to a focus on care, thus supporting the entire care process, including wellness and prevention (Nasi et al., 2015; Cucciniello et al., 2021). As such, mHealth stands as a revolutionary tool that underscores the significance of technology in enhancing accessibility and communication between service providers and users, expanding the app's capacity to gather information and reach a broader audience to strengthen existing services rather than creating entirely new ones (Millard, 2017).

Despite the abundant literature highlighting the potential of mHealth, evidence suggests low adoption rates among physicians and, particularly, patients (Tarricone et al., 2019). One contributing factor of this may be the frequent low quality of mHealth apps limiting clinician recommendations and patient use (Byambasuren et al., 2018). Moreover, most apps focus on conditions with significant global health burdens, such as diabetes (Cafazzo et al., 2012), mental health (Donker et al., 2013), and obesity (Turner et al., 2015), with relatively few targeting cancer (Nasi et al., 2015). At the heart of the app quality issue lies a design process that often neglects the needs of primary users, including patients and clinicians (Huckvale & Car, 2014).

5.1.2 Healthcare Service Design and Value Co-Creation through IT Interventions

Much of the existing service design research draws upon production and manufacturing metaphors, emphasising the streamlining, scripting, and standardisation of processes to minimise variations on the part of service providers (Stewart & Chase, 1999; Fitzsimmons & Fitzsimmon, 2004; Secchi et al., 2019). In this section, we approach patient care as a 'service'. Consequently, the section explores how patient care can add value to the lives of citizens and what the implications of this approach are for understanding their effectiveness. Our focus revolves around the resources dedicated to patient interaction and communication, with the goal of enhancing outcomes for both service providers and patients. Contemporary perspectives on value creation have evolved to recognise a more interconnected and dynamic environment (Lusch & Vargo, 2006). In healthcare, the interaction between service providers (e.g. medical specialists) and users (patients) has gained paramount significance (Joiner & Lusch, 2016).

The effective management of chronic diseases such as cancer hinges on collaborative interactions between individuals and their healthcare providers (Holman & Lorig, 2000). Technology-based interventions, including mobile technologies, serve as valuable enablers for direct, synchronous, and remote communication between physicians and patients, complementing face-to-face interactions in this dynamic setting. The adoption of such technologies transforms customers from passive recipients to active participants in the service delivery process (Prahalad & Ramaswamy, 2004).

This transformation holds particular significance in the healthcare sector, fundamentally altering the relationship and level of interaction between service providers (clinicians) and patients. Essentially, the digital exchange of health information between clinicians and patients, along with improved access to such information, facilitates the co-creation of value within the healthcare ecosystem. Devices such as mobile phones, which empower consumers to transmit information regarding their physiological functions and health-promoting activities as part of their daily lives, embody the essence of PSL by positioning the user as an active partner in value creation.

5.2 Research Method

In this subsection, we describe the research process, commencing with our initial intervention: the design of an mHealth app tailored for the case management of patients with lung cancer. The primary objective behind developing the mHealth app was to enhance communication between patients and healthcare providers, a factor consistently linked to improved patient outcomes and reductions in preventable expenditures, such as emergency department visits.

To construct the app, we followed several key steps:

1. We initiated the process by soliciting input from diverse stakeholders, including clinicians and patients with cancer. Additionally, we organised a workshop involving 100 international stakeholders to gather a wide range of perspectives.
2. We then proceeded with the development of the mHealth app, incorporating the insights and feedback obtained from stakeholders.

3. We conducted rigorous end-user testing to ensure the app's functionality and usability met the desired standards.
4. Finally, we evaluated the efficiency and efficacy of the app based on its performance in real-world scenarios.

Surprisingly, the initial mHealth app received a lukewarm reception not only from some newly onboarded research team members but also from our advisory clinicians, including five oncologists we had previously consulted. Both groups contended that significant revisions were necessary to make a meaningful contribution to both research and practical applications. To address these concerns and better serve the end-users, we received recommendations to broaden our stakeholder base. This involved engaging patients with cancer, as well as collaborating with new clinicians and patient advocacy groups, and expanding the scope of outcomes addressed by the app.

In alignment with this advice, we embarked on a second intervention, engaging in focus groups with severely ill patients with lung cancer.

These discussions prompted us to reflect critically on how we measure service quality and challenged our assumptions about who the primary end-user of the service is.

Following service design principles, we structured the revision process into four iterative phases:

1. *Stakeholder Re-engagement:* We expanded our engagement to include previously underrepresented voices – especially patients, caregivers, advocacy groups, and additional clinicians – to ensure a more holistic view of needs and expectations.
2. *Reassessment of Needs and Value Propositions*: We revisited our original design assumptions and gathered in-depth feedback on unmet needs, focusing on aspects such as usability, relevance of features, emotional burden, and clinical utility.
3. *Redesign and Prototyping*: Based on this feedback, we redefined core functionalities, prioritised features that directly addressed user pain points, and developed revised prototypes that better aligned with user journeys and decision-making processes.
4. *Testing and Iterative Refinement*: The revised prototypes were tested in low-fidelity and then medium-fidelity formats with target users, allowing for rapid cycles of feedback, refinement, and validation before final development.

This structured revision process not only improved the app's alignment with user needs but also reinforced the value of participatory service design in healthcare.

Rather than treating user input as an afterthought, we embedded it throughout the design cycle, ensuring that both patients and clinicians contributed meaningfully to the co-creation of a tool designed to support lung cancer care.

5.2.1 Design of LuCApp

To initiate the app's design phase, we solicited requirements. This involved conducting two surveys targeting two distinct populations of mHealth app stakeholders: randomly selected cancer clinicians and patients who utilise internet-enabled mobile devices such as smartphones. In the clinician survey, we assessed their perceptions of the operational implications of mHealth apps, particularly for those most directly impacted by clinicians' use of such apps (i.e. patients, clinicians, and hospitals). The survey results indicated that clinicians were most optimistic about the potential of mHealth apps to improve communication between patients and healthcare providers. However, on average, they perceived minimal benefits from these apps for both clinicians and patients.

The patient survey focused on assessing how the use of mHealth apps might impact the efforts of patients with cancer to manage their disease. Patients were queried about their perceptions of the potential benefits of mHealth app use in promoting healthy habits, improving diagnostics, enhancing data sharing, managing side effects, and, overall, improving their quality of life. The patients' responses indicated relative optimism about the potential of mHealth apps to enhance their quality of life. Nevertheless, on average, the patients did not strongly believe that app use would significantly improve their overall well-being.

The survey results underscored substantial room for enhancing the appeal of mHealth apps for both clinicians and patients. The project team gleaned crucial insights from the surveys, identifying several key elements relevant to app development. From the clinician's perspective, scepticism existed regarding the app's ability to reduce hospitalisation rates, enhance patient monitoring, reduce errors, increase patient attention, and alleviate side effects. On the patient front, confidence in the app's potential to improve diagnoses, facilitate data sharing, or manage treatment-based side effects was lacking.

To further delve into our survey findings, we organised an international workshop hosted at a prominent healthcare research centre in Europe. Over 100 stakeholders participated, including patient advocacy groups; clinicians; app developers; representatives from pharmaceutical, medical technology, and telecom industries; experts in medical communications and health education; payers; and policymakers. During the workshop, a member of the research team facilitated discussions on issues identified in the survey results. The participants provided valuable feedback concerning why patients and clinicians were not embracing mHealth apps, the main barriers hindering mHealth adoption in cancer care, and the potential impact of mHealth on clinician activities and patient quality of life.

Qualitative feedback from the workshop led us to identify three key themes that encapsulated the significance of user collaboration:

- *Desired characteristics of a cancer app*: Participants shared their perspectives on the essential attributes of an effective cancer app.
- *Lack of user-friendliness:* Existing mHealth apps were criticised for their inadequate integration into work and life contexts, leading to difficulties in usability.
- *Poorly designed interfaces:* Participants emphasised the need for more user-friendly interfaces in mHealth apps.

Building on this feedback, we organised a roundtable discussion involving four representatives from leading patient and clinician associations in Europe and the United States. This roundtable served as a platform to solicit feedback on designing an mHealth app that better aligned with user needs. We leveraged insights from the workshop to formulate a set of questions for the roundtable participants. A team member moderated the discussion, which was recorded and later transcribed for analysis. Probing questions (primarily revolving around three central themes: information content, interface design and usability) were utilised to elicit suggestions from the participants.

Stakeholders unanimously concurred that current mHealth app developers often overlook the needs and expectations of patients, resulting in app functionalities that fail to meet user expectations. The participants stressed the importance of identifying target audience preferences and requirements as a fundamental step in app design. Key considerations included understanding the characteristics of the main target population (e.g. age, disease type and stage, and familiarity with technology), using simple and accessible language and optimising the app's layout for ease of use.

To further refine our app design requirements, we engaged with clinicians, whom we regarded as valuable sources of educational content and insights into lung cancer symptoms. We conducted five in-depth interviews with oncologists from various Italian hospitals, whom we referred to as advisory clinicians, given their ongoing involvement in our research. These interviews, lasting approximately 60 minutes each, were recorded and analysed by two independent coders using content analysis to identify core themes. The clinicians emphasised the importance of specific, straightforward content with minimal medical jargon, short and direct paragraphs/sentences and precise targeting of the app's intended user population. As previously noted, most mHealth apps suffer from a lack of specificity, and the clinicians' input aided us in identifying a specific subgroup of patients with cancer who could benefit from the app: those diagnosed with small or non-small cell lung cancer eligible for chemotherapy, immunotherapy or biological therapy.

5.2.2 Developing LuCApp 1.0

Upon gathering the necessary requirements, we commenced the development of LuCApp. Based on a comprehensive examination of emerging themes from the survey, workshop, roundtable, and expert interviews, we structured our design guidelines into three categories: design process, functionality and usefulness. Figure 2 provides a snapshot of the app's main screen, highlighting its key elements. LuCApp also incorporates automatic alerts, reminders and tips that complement the patient's therapy. The app offers two modes: clinician mode and patient mode.

Involving Stakeholders Using a Service Design Approach

Following the completion of the initial version of LuCApp, we conducted a series of focus groups to assess and refine the app further.

Initial Feedback from Advisory Clinicians via Focus Group

For the initial focus group, we revisited our advisory clinicians to present our prototype.

Following the approach outlined by Tremblay and colleagues (Tremblay et al., 2010a), which leverages focus groups to evaluate an IT artefact, we opted not to test the app in real use but to employ the focus groups as partial field tests for assessing proposed designs and features with stakeholders. This approach, as noted by van Aken et al. (2016), can yield valuable insights and lead to more relevant management implications. This approach has been validated in various research projects (e.g. Aier et al., 2011; Miah & Mckay, 2014; Prat et al., 2015; Recker & Mendling, 2016) and also allowed direct interaction with the central target populations of LuCApp, facilitating probing on functionality and usefulness.

Before each focus group, moderators introduced the app, outlined the objectives and provided general information about the focus group. The planning process included creating a script (Tremblay et al., 2012) to probe participants for

- suggestions for improving the current app version and
- feedback on how clinicians' use of LuCApp in managing patients with cancer could impact patient health monitoring, evaluation and overall decision-making.

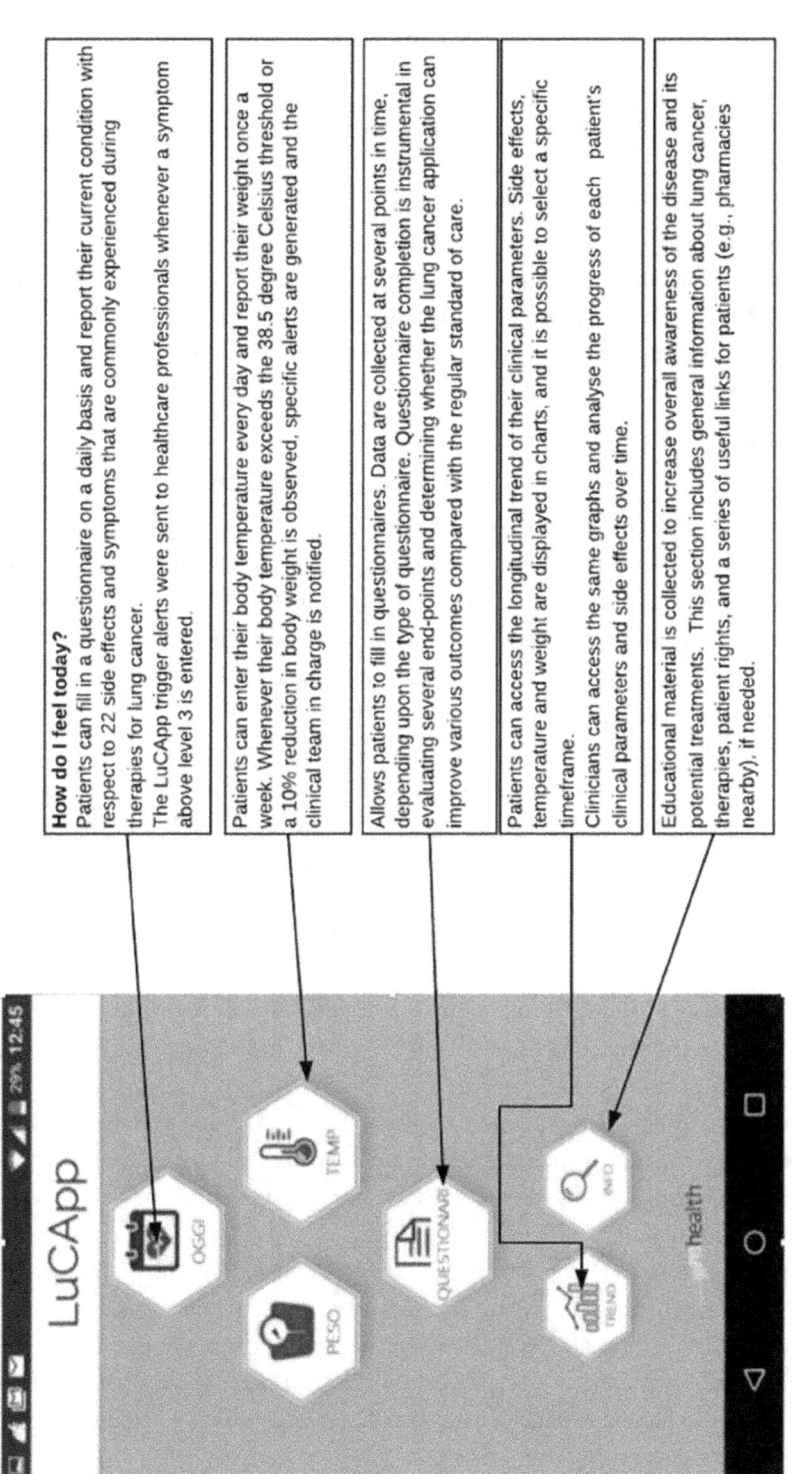

Figure 2 Screenshot of LuCApp

Qualitative analysis of the focus group responses highlighted four primary concerns raised by clinicians, including

(i) doubts about LuCApp's differentiation from existing apps or those documented in prior research,
(ii) lack of clear evidence supporting LuCApp's potential to enhance efficacy and efficiency,
(iii) uncertainty regarding how LuCApp could benefit both clinicians and patients in lung cancer disease management and
(iv) concerns, particularly among the elderly, about potential challenges in using the app.

Involving a New Group of Clinicians

The concerns raised by our advisory clinicians were pivotal to our process. Recognising the need for more stakeholder input to improve the mHealth app, we assembled a new panel of clinicians. This panel consisted of oncologists who had not previously interacted with our research team or LuCApp but possessed familiarity with the mHealth app environment and could potentially become users of the proposed mHealth app.

This group of clinicians appreciated the real-time information provided by patients about their symptoms and severity, enabling swift contact with patients and immediate suggestions for next steps. They found the trend component of the app significant (see Figure 2). However, they recommended removing this functionality from the patient's version of the app due to concerns that observing negative trends could distress and demoralise patients if their conditions did not improve over time. One clinician (C1) articulated this concern as follows: 'Displaying side effects, temperature and weight in the charts can influence the patient's behaviour and have a negative impact on their quality of life' (C1)

Another participant (C2) noted that the app could revolutionise current practices, as clinicians often communicate with patients through email and WhatsApp, leading to fragmented conversations; LuCApp offers a more systematic, innovative, and efficient solution.

A participant (C4) stressed the importance of considering the disease stage and type, as patients with severe symptoms might struggle to use LuCApp independently as their conditions worsen. Simplifying the symptom descriptions for easy recognition and accessibility was also recommended by clinicians. This experience underscored the value of involving experts in the process to enhance utility and user-friendliness.

Engaging with Patients with Lung Cancer through Focus Groups for the Design of LuCApp

Initially, we had reservations about engaging with patients with lung cancer due to their challenging circumstances: they were often seriously ill and nearing the end of life. However, we recognised the importance of enhancing patient and family engagement in self-care and streamlining care and communication, especially for high-need, high-cost populations. Therefore, we embarked on the demanding task of recruiting and conducting focus groups with patients to enhance our app.

Conversations with patients shed light on functionalities that could provide reassurance to patients, their families, and their caregivers while also improving communication with clinicians. One patient aptly described the app as follows:

> 'This app reminds me of a great diary that I could fill in every day and share in real-time with my clinicians.' (Pt1)

The patients emphasised the significance of symptom monitoring, recognising that it could collect data to enhance not only their treatment plans but also those of other current and future patients.

The patients also shared that LuCApp instilled a sense of security in them as it allowed them to report their symptoms in real time, particularly when they were mild or moderate, which could be indicators of serious issues that might otherwise go unreported to clinicians. The participants believed this reporting could advance medical knowledge, offering insights into when mild or moderate symptoms might lead to adverse outcomes. One patient put it succinctly: 'I think the app helps me to feel safer, not only because I know I am being followed by the doctor but also because I can see that clinical research is moving forward. We all hope, or at least I hope, not so much to heal but to stop the disease ...' (Pt3).

A crucial revelation emerged regarding how LuCApp affected the relationship between patients and their caregivers. Participants noted that caregivers, often attentive to their loved ones' needs and health, could benefit from LuCApp as a tool to stay informed about the patient's health conditions. Some suggested creating a login ID and password for caregivers to access vital patient care information. This feature would be particularly reassuring when caregivers were spouses or children.

The patients believed that LuCApp could enhance their relationship with clinicians by providing real-time access to all relevant data and information in one place, improving the signal-to-noise ratio. While they understood that the app couldn't replace in-person visits, they felt it would keep clinicians better informed about their well-being. As one patient said, 'It will be like having the doctor with me at home all day long!' (Pt2).

This highlighted the promising role of technology in healthcare as a secure and easily accessible tool to enhance communication between patients and doctors.

Furthermore, when asked about LuCApp's potential impact on the overall care process, the patients saw its value in sharing information about their conditions and symptoms among different healthcare organisations and clinicians, including general practitioners and specialised oncologists.

These valuable insights from the patient focus groups challenged our previous assumptions and contradicted the opinions of some expert clinicians and existing research on clinician–patient interactions. This led us to reassess our understanding of using IT for lung cancer care. Enabling patients and clinicians to co-create value in unexpected ways suggests that intentionally involving challenging-to-reach clients, such as severely ill patients, in the service development process may be the key to enhancing service provision.

Redefining Quality of Life as a Healthcare Service Outcome: Success and Value Co-Creation through mHealth

Our engagement with patients with lung cancer through focus groups not only challenged the perspectives of some expert clinicians but also contradicted previous research on clinician–patient interactions (Min et al., 2014; Sundberg et al., 2017; Uhm et al., 2017). Reflecting on these disparities between clinicians and patients forced us to question our initial assumptions regarding IT-based care management for lung cancer. We revised and refined our understanding of how an IT intervention can be utilised to manage patient care and reshape the design and use of an mHealth app. This process enabled patients and clinicians to co-create value in unforeseen ways, emphasising the importance of actively involving challenging-to-serve clients, such as severely ill patients, in the service development process to enhance service delivery.

5.3 Discussion and Conclusions

In conclusion, this section underscored the pivotal role of both patients and front-line healthcare professionals within service organisations – particularly in healthcare – where their actions and interactions are integral to the service production process. There is a growing imperative to consider the individual needs and preferences of patients to ensure efficient and effective care delivery. This recognition positions the patient as a central actor in the design and management of healthcare systems, as emphasised by Bretthauer and Savin (2018).

Information and communication technologies (ICTs) are reshaping customer experiences during service encounters and their interactions with service providers, echoing the insights of Scherer et al. (2015). Customers have evolved from passive recipients to active participants in the process of service delivery, aligning with the concepts put forth by Prahalad and Ramaswamy (2004). This transformation underscores the changing dynamics of service interactions and the evolving role of customers in shaping the service landscape.

5.3.1 Observation 1: Unlocking Collaborative Value Creation: The Transformative Role of mHealth Apps in Healthcare

Our initial insight in this context highlights the pivotal role of technologies such as mHealth apps in facilitating collaborative value creation between customers (patients) and service providers (clinicians). Our focus group findings underscore that the flexible interactions enabled by the mHealth app not only enhance patients' perception of their treatment and well-being but also equip clinicians with valuable insights for better patient care. The in-depth data on treatment and treatment response significantly improves patients' overall outlook. By mitigating information imbalances between clinicians and patients, LuCApp empowers patients to engage in discussions at a higher level of sophistication than previously anticipated by clinicians. The app essentially facilitates deeper clinician–patient interactions, leading to a shift in clinicians' perception of patients' level of health literacy. This initial observation underscores the potential of ICT in public service delivery and highlights the transformative impact it can have on service enhancement by addressing customers' accessibility and usability needs.

5.3.2 Observation 2: Inclusive Service Design: Leveraging Extreme Customer Cases for Enhanced Service Delivery

The second significant insight from this section revolves around the emphasis on the selection of customer types to be included in the service design process. Extensive research has examined service systems in which rational customers make decisions based on service quality. However, these studies often overlook the scenario where patients exhibit significant heterogeneity, as is often the case with chronic patient treatments (Rajan et al., 2019). As discussed earlier, many design processes tend to cater to the preferences of the median, average or typical customer. Unfortunately, this approach frequently sidelines the most vulnerable consumers, exacerbating disparities in healthcare (Joiner & Lusch, 2016).

To foster customer empowerment and accommodation and to address customer diversity (Beltagui et al., 2016), we deliberately focused on extreme customer cases – in this instance, patients with lung cancer, many of whom were in advanced stages of their illness. Surprisingly, these individuals expressed optimism about the potential impact of the mHealth app, which we designed with their active involvement. The transformative potential of technology-mediated service interventions is not evenly distributed among all customer segments – certain customers experience a more pronounced impact than others. Moreover, the demands placed on service delivery processes are not uniform across the entire customer population.

In this context, designing services and interventions, such as mHealth apps, that explicitly consider the needs of customers who are traditionally harder to serve may prove to be a more efficient allocation of resources than focusing solely on customers clustered around the centre of the distribution. In essence, accounting for the perspectives of extreme customers during the service design phase could enable organisations to allocate resources in a manner that enhances service delivery for all customer types.

5.3.3 Observation 3: Role of mHealth Apps in Healthcare: Shaping the Future of Patient-Centric Service Design

Our third contribution lies in the formulation of testable propositions, which serve as a foundation for empirically grounded research questions. These propositions allowed us to refine and rectify our understanding of the problem context. Although the emerging insights are not universally applicable (Browning & de Treville, 2018), they guide us towards testable propositions within the realm of mHealth app usage. Similar to the work of Aime et al. (2014) and Collins and Browning (2019), our research in this section unveils and suggests propositions rather than conducting formal hypothesis testing.

In summary, this section provided a glimpse into the transformative potential of an IT intervention, LuCApp, within the healthcare sector, particularly among severely ill patients with lung cancer. It underscored the notion that, when assessing service outcomes, the most favourable results may encompass not only cost savings but also an enhanced quality of life for patients. The insights garnered from focus group interviews mark a significant step towards unravelling the intricacies of effective treatment for severely ill patients with lung cancer. The rigorous utilisation of focus groups as a qualitative research method (Tremblay et al., 2010a) in user interviews involving both patients and clinicians illuminated unexpected elements that contribute to the generation of new knowledge during interventionist research. Furthermore, the advent of mobile technologies and, more recently, wearable devices has enabled service organisations to forge personalised interactions with a diverse customer base on a much larger scale (Kim & Lee, 2017).

Thus, this section delved into the impact of mHealth apps on patients with cancer and their healthcare providers, exploring how these technologies can shape patient well-being. Insights gleaned from focus group interviews with clinicians and patients shed light on potential modifications to the design process employed in mHealth app development, ultimately enhancing the value of such apps for both service organisations, particularly those in the healthcare sector, and their users (in this context, patients with cancer).

6 What Is Next for the Future of Public Service Design?

New Public Management (NPM) has had significant implications for the field of public management, largely due to the discussions it provoked regarding how to effectively create value for service users (Hood, 1991). Many of these discussions centred around the concepts of public value and tailoring service provision to meet the specific needs and demands of users. While NPM's approach, which relied heavily on generic market mechanisms, has been widely criticised for an overly reductionist perspective (Dunleavy & Hood, 1994), the broader shift towards prioritising service users and creating public value represents an important evolution in public management research and practice. In this context, the application of service design principles to public management has emerged as an important response to NPM's espoused reductionist perspective, because of its efforts to embrace the distinctiveness of the public sector context (Osborne, 2010).

Efforts to implement a service design approach to developing and delivering public services call for a closer examination of who uses public services and how to increase the value proposition for these users (Stickdorn & Schneider, 2011). The service design paradigm proposes that this aim is best achieved through the co-creation of public services, where service users and service providers are actively involved in the design of public services (Manzini & Jegou, 2003). To this end, service design is important not just because it offers a methodology for grounding the design of public services in the lived experiences of the users they target, but also because of the insights it offers into managing the complexity of public service provision.

At the same time, while research on service design offers important insight into solving the conceptual problem of enhancing the value proposition of public services for service users, this line of research is still in its early stages of development and therefore leaves many important implementation questions unanswered. The purpose of this Element is to contribute to the advancement of service design research in two key ways. First, in Sections 1 and 2 we review existing public administration and management research on service design to provide an overview of the current state of the art. Section 1 offers readers an overview of service design research within the broader context of approaches to improving public service delivery and offers insight into the different components. Section 2 elaborates on the user-centred approach embodied by service design theory and reviews approaches to design services using the user-centred approach.

Second, across three empirical studies, we provide novel evidence that helps address existing gaps in understanding in terms of how to implement service design in ways that improve value for public service users.

In Section 3, we explored efforts to redesign municipal public services in the wake of the COVID-19 pandemic. As we illustrate, public experiences with the pandemic have had a substantive influence on service delivery expectations and priorities. These shifts, in turn, have forced governments to reconsider service delivery mechanisms with a particular emphasis on digital platforms. Through interviews with service providers, we demonstrate that a crucial aspect of effectively transitioning to digital platforms is for service providers to account for how service expectations have changed in an increasingly digital context and, in turn, how this shift will influence determinants of satisfaction. However, we also find that the importance of directly engaging with citizens to discover how their preferences have shifted is overlooked, which, in turn contributes to misaligned service reforms. Crucially, through our interviews with service providers and users, we find that a key challenge relates to balancing public demands for more innovative and responsive service delivery with the everyday realities of service provision. However, engaging with the public early on in the service design process offers a promising path towards effectively navigating this tension in ways that improve value for service users, while also enabling service providers to operating within existing performance constraints. Cumulatively, Section 3 suggests that in the wake of major social events, co-creation and co-design offer a vital path toward understanding how service expectations have evolved and instituting service reforms that effectively respond to these shifts.

Section 4 uses a survey to identify which municipal services citizens are least satisfied with, which in our case was education, and then, based on these findings, leverages interview data from school children's parents and service providers to better understand ways of improving satisfaction. Through interviews with parents and service users we again identify a mismatch in terms of what service users demand and how the government attempts to meet those demands. Specifically, a major source of dissatisfaction for parents was an ostensible lack of transparency on the part of schools in terms of what children were doing while in school. From the standpoint of the school, a key mechanism for enhancing transparency was detailed diaries children kept daily documenting what children did at school; School administrators were unaware that this tool was unpopular with parents. All told, Section 4 illustrates how the service design perspective and input from service users can be leveraged to pinpoint critical aspects of service delivery and to iteratively identify interventions that are capable of enhancing value.

In Section 5 we examine factors contributing to value creation for a distinct type of service user – patients with lung cancer – through the development of a mobile health application that intends to help them communicate with their healthcare provider and manage their symptoms. Through focus groups with clinicians tasked with caring for these patients and the patients themselves, we again uncover crucial gaps. We find that clinicians lacked an understanding of how knowledgeable patients were in terms of their condition and related terminology and that patients felt that the resulting superficial communication impeded their ability to manage their condition. To this end, using the app to enable more in-depth discussions regarding symptoms, conditions, and potential interventions would significantly improve the value this app creates for the end user. We also find that existing mobile design frameworks, which emphasised the median or modal user, were poorly suited to address the needs of patients with lung cancer, which represent a more extreme type of user. Through such insights, we learned patients with lung cancer expressed a desire to engage with the platform than would have otherwise been expected, in large part because of the value they believed it offered them to improve their condition and create a sense of community with others who are also experiencing this condition. Findings from Section 5 highlight the value of tailoring design processes to the specific needs and experiences of diverse user populations, such as vulnerable patients, to truly enhance service provision and value creation.

Across these three empirical sections, we also find four important commonalities.

First, they demonstrate significant mismatches between service providers and users, with service providers often making incorrect inferences regarding the needs and preferences of service users. Importantly, these incorrect inferences are consequential in that we find they consistently contribute to user discontent. At the same time, they can be resolved by involving service users in the service design process. Second, our findings show that user preferences are not stable over time, but rather can change in the event of major social or live events. This highlights the iterative nature of service design and the importance of co-design and co-creation as a process to guide the evolution of service provision to ensure continual value creation of users. It also means that co-creation and co-design constitute frameworks to ensure the continued relevance of public services in a continuously evolving world. Third, we demonstrate the importance of recognising the diversity of different populations of service users. Different groups expect and demand different things from government, and it is only through intentionally engaging with different users that different aspects of service design, such as co-creation or co-design, will be able to broaden the value proposition for public services. In short, to make service design more inclusive, efforts must be made not just to engage with the modal or average user, but also more extreme cases. A final key finding across our empirical sections is that technology is consistently flagged as a resource to facilitate the interactions between service users and providers. Here, the emphasis is placed in particular upon technology not solely as a means of providing services, but also as a tool to make it easier for the two parties to exchange information in terms of performance and user needs.

What do these findings mean for an emerging body of service design research in public administration and public management field? In the remaining subsections of this concluding section, we outline two key contributions of this Element the first for efforts to advance a citizen-centred strategic orientation in public service design and a second regarding the importance of digital technologies as a means of improving feedback loops between service providers and users.

6.1 Advancing a Citizens-Centred Strategic Orientation for Public Service Design Research

While service design research emphasises user engagement in different stages of service provision, what remains unclear is just what types of value citizen-centred service design creates and for whom. Specifically, as discussed in Sections 1 and 2, a key theme in service design research is that through the use of co-design and co-creation techniques, service providers are able to engage with service users to align different aspects of a service with user preferences and needs. Yet as we also discuss, user preferences vary in time and by group. This variation makes the implementation of a citizen-centred strategic orientation in the service design process fraught by questions over implementation such as who to involve and when. Importantly, findings from our empirical sections help to address some of these important implementation questions that were identified in Sections 1 and 2. They do so in two keyways. First, noting the tendency for user preferences and needs to change over time, our findings highlight the importance of repeated exchanges between service providers and users. Co-design plays a crucial role in aligning assumptions regarding service provision between these two entities, and co-creation establishes a forum for iterative exchanges to ensure that service provision evolves in ways that continue to create value for users. Our findings help contribute toward a more strategic approach to engaging service users in co-design and co-creation by illustrating how significant events, at either the individual or the society level can result in a shift in user expectations and, in turn, a demand for modified service provision. Thus, in order to ensure that services evolve in ways that continue to create value, a key implication of our findings is that service providers must focus on creating processes to continual solicit feedback from users who are experiencing significant life events (e.g. having children, retirement, or experiencing illness) and also to create feedback loops for irregular societal events, such as, in our case, the COVID-19 pandemic. All told, to advance a citizen-centred strategic orientation, service providers must create different mechanisms to capture evolving expectations of service users, once focused on predictable, yet significant, life events and a second that focuses on societal events that are more difficult to predict.

From the standpoint of public service design research, the potential for different paths to ensure a given service continues to create value for users breaks ground on new directions for future research. One important area that deserves further attention concerns the implications of different approaches to co-design and creation for social equity and inclusive public service provision. While studies have highlighted the importance of incorporating user feedback into service design and provision, past evidence suggests that doing so often benefits the affluent at the expense of those who are less affluent (Holbein, 2016; Porumbescu et al., 2021; Osborne et al., 2022b). The possibility of strategically incorporating groups into the processes of co-design and co-creation creates the potential to mitigate this reinforcement effect. However, important questions remain. For example, given that biases in service provision are complex and a function of historic disparities and current life circumstances, which groups stand to benefit from inclusion in co-design and co-creation processes is an important question to be explored by future research. Put differently, while co-design and co-creation are powerful tools in improving the value of public services, further research is needed to understand which types of service biases are capable of mitigating. Relatedly, future studies that employ mixed methods designs capable of leveraging insights from focus groups as well as quantitative data to assess impact are needed.

A second important area for further research in the realm of a citizen-centred strategic orientation are the legal and political dimensions of representation within service design processes. Specifically, while service providers and service users may both desire to collaborate on the design and provision of public services, politics, laws, and regulations may make these forms of collaboration difficult. For example, the provision of means-tested benefits are heavily regulated and, as a result, may offer limited opportunities for service users to engage in co-design activities with service providers in ways that meaningfully influence the value created by these services for users (Moynihan et al., 2015). Furthermore, political dynamics can influence the distribution of power and resources within service design processes, potentially marginalising certain groups from meaningful participation (Arnstein, 1969). In some cases, entrenched interests or power structures may prioritise the perspectives of specific stakeholders over others, leading to unequal representation in co-design initiatives (cf. Clark, 2022a). Additionally, the political climate surrounding public services may create formal or informal barriers to participation for marginalised or underrepresented communities, further exacerbating existing disparities in service provision. Understanding these political dynamics is crucial for developing strategies to promote inclusivity and equity in co-design efforts, ensuring that all voices are heard and valued in the design and delivery of public services.

6.2 Using Digital Technologies to Engage Vulnerable Groups

Determining who to bring to the table and when are important elements of service design theory; however, an issue that has received less attention is how. The question of how to mediate interactions between service users and providers is important because it influences the resources individuals need to participate and, as such, helps determine who can participate in co-design and co-creation initiatives. Put differently, mediums used to facilitate engagement between service providers and users have important implications for the value service design creates. As prior research documents, in person participation mechanisms, that require individuals to be physically present at a particular place and time require a relatively significant amount of resources from members of vulnerable groups (Fung, 2015). Given the significant resource demands, members of these groups often opt out of participating (Delli Carpini & Keeter, 1996).

Technology is often discussed as a means of alleviating these resource constraints and, by doing so, empowering members of vulnerable groups to be heard (Bimber, 2001). Indeed, there is a growing body of research on digital coproduction, with research in this vein frequently documenting the potential to ensure the needs of more vulnerable groups are being addressed (Clark et al., 2020; Osborne et al., 2021; Young, 2022). However, research on the potential for digital tools to facilitate co-design and co-creation remains limited. Our findings help to address this gap, with evidence across all three studies documenting the potential of technology to improve interactions between service users and providers, and for this relationship to be strongest among members of more vulnerable groups. Our findings dovetail with previous research highlighting the mobilising potential of digital technologies, but also shed light on important implications in terms of how to leverage these tools to improve the value proposition that results from service design theory. One implication concerns the potential of technology to alleviate resource constraints the keep members of vulnerable groups from participating in processes. While research on digital coproduction has shown how technology can enable members of vulnerable groups to actively participate in service delivery by, for example, uploading pictures of service issues in their community, we show that digital platforms can facilitate participation among members of these groups throughout the entire service lifecycle. This is important because it has profound implications for the value co-design and co-creation. A second key implication of our findings concerns the importance of using technology can play in fostering more inclusive public service design. As we document, mismatches are commonplace, where service providers often make incorrect assumptions about user needs and demands. These incorrect assumptions have significant negative implications for service delivery, especially for members of groups with special needs. To this end, the use of technology to make it easier for members of vulnerable groups to participate in co-design can help to ensure services are designed in ways that promote inclusion and social equity.

These implications also create opportunities for new research. One area requiring further research concerns understanding what vulnerable groups digital platforms can enable participation in co-design and co-creation for. Specifically, determinants of participation are complex and while resources are important, so are other factors such as perceptions of self-efficacy and trust in government (Shim & Park, 2016b; Clark, 2018; Mergel et al., 2021). Both perceptions of self-efficacy and trust in government tend to be lower for members of vulnerable groups, meaning that the lack of engagement, at least for some groups (cf. Cutrona et al., 2000). This implies that efforts to reduce resources members of vulnerable groups need to engage with service providers, on their own, may not be enough. That is, digital platforms may not be a silver bullet for engaging all vulnerable groups in co-design and co-creation and, by extension, contributing to inclusive service provision among all entities that have difficulty having their voices heard. However, they do have the potential to improve representation of some groups. To this end, further research is needed to understand which groups stand to benefit from the use of digital platforms and which groups other interventions are needed.

A second area that would benefit from further research concerns efforts to refine our understanding of the types of digital platforms that can enable participation in co-design and co-creation. As technology evolves, so too do the ways individuals can interact with government, from synchronous to asynchronous, from video-based communication to text-based interactions. A key question that emanates from this diversity is just what features, and technologies more generally are most effective at engaging service users. A related point is that answers to this question will inevitably depend on specific groups. For example, individuals who have difficulty expressing themselves verbally may feel more comfortable with platforms that enable text-based interactions, whereas the elderly may feel more reassured by platforms that enable video or synchronous forms of engagement. All told, more research is needed to develop a more systematic understanding of what types of technologies are most effective for whom when attempting to foster greater and more inclusive engagement in co-design and creation.

6.3 A Vision for the Future of Public Service Practice

As this Element has demonstrated, the integration of service design principles into public service delivery is not merely a methodological refinement – it represents a deeper reorientation of public service practice around the lived realities of those it seeks to serve. The evidence presented across our empirical sections reveals that service design offers a powerful framework for making public services more inclusive, adaptive, and responsive. Looking forward, we see five core principles that should guide the future practice of public service design:

1. *From Users to Co-Producers*: Public services must increasingly treat citizens not simply as end-users but as co-producers of value. This implies early and sustained engagement in the design and delivery of services, recognising the expertise users bring from lived experience. Co-design and co-creation are not add-ons but foundational to achieving relevance and legitimacy in public service delivery.
2. *Embrace of Iteration and Flexibility*: As our findings show, user needs are not static – they evolve with personal life events and broader societal shifts. Future public services must embed continuous feedback mechanisms and

iterative processes, allowing services to adapt over time. Flexibility must become a core design criterion, not an exception.
3. *Equity through Intentional Inclusion*: Service design must actively resist the tendency to default to the 'average user' and instead foreground diversity – particularly among vulnerable or underserved groups. This requires targeted outreach, accessible engagement formats, and inclusive design processes that recognise different forms of participation.
4. *Technology as Enabler, Not Solution*: Digital platforms hold real promise for improving participation and service responsiveness, but their effectiveness depends on thoughtful, user-centred implementation. Future public service practice must focus on matching technological tools with the capabilities, preferences, and constraints of different user groups – especially those historically excluded.
5. *Culture Change in Public Institutions*: To embed service design meaningfully, a shift in organisational culture is needed. This includes valuing user insight as strategic knowledge, legitimising experimentation and iteration, and building the capabilities of public managers to facilitate participatory design processes. Leadership must model and support this shift.

In sum, the future of public service practice lies not in adopting a single method or technology but in embracing a relational, participatory, and iterative mindset. Service design, when understood in this broader sense, offers a pathway to reinvigorate public services as spaces of shared value creation – responsive to real needs, grounded in trust, and committed to equity.

Public managers, policymakers, and researchers alike must collaborate to move this vision forward – not only by advancing service design as a toolkit, but by fostering the institutional conditions in which meaningful co-creation can flourish.

References

Adlin, T., & Pruitt, J. S. (2010). *The Essential Persona Lifecycle: Your Guide to Building and Using Personas. Elsevier eBooks*. Elsevier BV. https://doi.org/10.1016/c2009-0-62475-2.

Aier, S., Fischer, C., & Winter, R. (2011). Construction and evaluation of a meta-model for enterprise architecture design principles. *Proceedings of the 10th International Conference on Wirtschaftsinformatik*, 1–11.

Aime, F., Humphrey, S., DeRue, D. S., & Paul, J. B. (2014). The riddle of heterarchy: Power transitions in cross-functional teams. *Academy of Management Journal*, 57(2), 327–352.

Alves, H., Fernandes, C., & Raposo, M. (2016). Value co-creation: Concept and contexts of application and study. *Journal of Business Research*, 69(5), 1626–1633.

American Cancer Society. (2024). Cancer Facts & Figures 2024. Atlanta: American Cancer Society. www.cancer.org.

American Lung Association. (2023). State of Lung Cancer Report. www.lung.org.

Andreassen, T. W., Lervik-Olsen, L., & Snyder, H. (2016). The role of co-design and value creation in service design. *Journal of Service Theory and Practice*, 26(1), 123–134.

Arnstein, S. R. (1969). A ladder of citizen participation. *Journal of the American Planning Association*, 35(4), 216–224.

Auh, S., Bell, S. J., McLeod, C. S., & Shih, E. (2007). Co-production and customer loyalty in financial services. *Journal of Retailing*, 83(3), 359–370. https://doi.org/10.1016/j.jretai.2007.03.001.

Bason, C. (2017). *Leading Public Design: Discovering Human-Centred Governance*. Policy Press.

Bason, C. (2010). *Leading Public Sector Innovation: Co-creating for a Better Society*. Bristol: Policy Press.

Bason, C., & Austin, R. D. (2019). Design for the public sector. *Administrative Sciences*, 9(1), 1727–1757.

Bellé, N., Belardinelli, P., Cucciniello, M., & Nasi, G. (2023). Experimental evidence on the determinants of citizens' expectations toward public services. *Public Administration Review*, 27(5), 751–772.

Beltagui, A., Candi, M., & Riedel, J. C. K. H. (2016). Setting the stage for service experience: Design strategies for functional services. *Journal of Service Management*, 27(5), 751–772.

Bimber, B. (2001). Information and political engagement in America: The search for effects of information technology at the individual level. *Political Research Quarterly*, 54(1), 53–67.

Bitner, M. J. (1992). Servicescapes: The impact of physical surroundings on customers and employees. *Journal of Marketing*, 56(2), 57–71.

Bitner, M. J., Booms, B. H., & Tetreault, M. S. (1990). The service encounter: Diagnosing favorable and unfavorable incidents. *Journal of Marketing*, 54(1), 71–84. https://doi.org/10.2307/1252174.

Bitner, M. J., Ostrom, A. L., & Morgan, F. N. (2008). Service blueprinting: A practical technique for service innovation. *California Management Review*, 50(3), 66–94.

Björgvinsson, E., Ehn, P., & Hillgren, P.-A. (2012). Design things and design thinking: Contemporary participatory design challenges. *Design Issues*, 28(3), 101–116.

Blomkamp, E. (2018). The promise of co-design for public policy. *Australian Journal of Public Administration*, 77(4), 729–743.

Bluethmann, S. M., Mariotto, A. B., & Rowland, J. H. (2016). Anticipating the 'Silver Tsunami': Prevalence trajectories and comorbidity burden among older cancer survivors in the United States. *Cancer Epidemiology, Biomarkers & Prevention*, 25(7), 1029–1036.

Bouckaert, G., & Van de Walle, S. (2003). Comparing measures of citizen trust and user satisfaction as indicators of 'good governance': Difficulties in linking trust and satisfaction indicators. *International Review of Administrative Sciences*, 69(3), 329–343.

Bovaird, T., & Loeffler, E. (2012). From engagement to co-production: The contribution of users and communities to outcomes and public value. *Voluntas* 23, 1119–1138. https://doi.org/10.1007/s11266-012-9309-6

Bretthauer, S. T., & Savin, S. (2018). Efficient frontier of outcomes: Evidence from the VA's MOVE! Weight Management Program. *Health Services Research*, 53(3), 1752–1776.

Brown, T. (2008). Design thinking. *Harvard Business Review*, 86(6), 84–92.

Browning, T. R., & de Treville, S. (2018). Process model payoff. *Management Science*, 64(4), 1595–1618.

Byambasuren, O., Sanders, S., Beller, E., & Glasziou, P. (2018). Prescribable mHealth apps identified from an overview of systematic reviews. *NPJ Digital Medicine*, 1, 12. https://www.nature.com/articles/s41746-018-0021-9.

Cafazzo, J. A., Casselman, M., Hamming, N., Katzman, D. K., & Palmert, M. R. (2012). Design of an mHealth app for the self-management of adolescent type 1 diabetes: A pilot study. *Journal of Medical Internet Research*, 14(3), e70. https://pubmed.ncbi.nlm.nih.gov/22564332/.

References

Calde, S. J., Goodwin, K., & Reimann, R. (2002). Strategies for integrating user experience into software development. *Interactions*, 9(6), 12–23.

Chen, J., Haddad, D., Selsky, J. et al. (2012). Making sense of mobile health data: An open architecture to improve individual- and population-level health. *Journal of Medical Internet Research*, 14(4), e112. https://pubmed.ncbi.nlm.nih.gov/22875563/.

Christensen, T., & Lægreid, P. (2007). The whole-of-government approach to public sector reform. *Public Administration Review*, 67, 1059–1066. 10.1111/j.1540-6210.2007.00797.x.

Chun, S. A., Shulman, S., Sandoval, R., & Hovy, E. (2010). Government 2.0: Making connections between citizens, data and government. *Information Polity*, 15(1/2), 1–9.

Clark, J. K. (2017). Designing public participation: Managing problem settings and social equity. *Public Administration Review*, 78(3), 362–374. https://doi.org/10.1111/puar.12872.

Clark, G. (2018). Trust in government and willingness to participate in co-design activities. *Public Management Review*, 20(5), 647–666.

Clark, J. K. (2022a). Equitable deliberative participation design: A call to use a lens of multidimensional power. *Perspectives on Public Management and Governance*, 5(3), 204–208. https://doi.org/10.1093/ppmgov/gvac011.

Clark, T. N. (2022b). The power dynamics in public service co-design: An analysis. *Journal of Public Administration Research and Theory*, 32(1), 95–110.

Clark, G., Brudney, J. L., & Jang, S. G. (2020). Coproduction of government services and the new information technology: Investigating the distributional biases. *Public Administration Review*, 80(4), 540–551.

Clark, B. Y., Brudney, J. L., Jang, S.-G., & Davy, B. (2019). Do advanced information technologies produce equitable government responses in coproduction: An examination of 311 systems in 15 U.S. cities. *The American Review of Public Administration*, 50(3), 315–327. https://doi.org/10.1177/0275074019894564.

Clarke, A., & Craft, J. (2018). The twin faces of public sector design. *Government Information Quarterly*, 35(3), 339–347.

Collins, C. J., & Browning, B. (2019). The making of a leader: Implications of leadership development for early career outcomes. *The Leadership Quarterly*, 30(4), 488–501.

Cooper, A. (1999). *The Inmates Are Running the Asylum: Why High Tech Products Drive Us Crazy and How to Restore the Sanity*. Indianapolis, IN: Sams-Pearson Education.

Cooper, A., Reimann, R., Cronin, D., & Noessel, C. (2014). *About Face: The Essentials of Interaction Design* (4th ed.). Indianapolis, IN: Wiley.

Creswell, J. W., & Plano Clark, V. L. (2007). *Designing and Conducting Mixed Methods Research*. Thousand Oaks, CA:Sage.

Cucciniello, M., Porumbescu, G. A., & Grimmelikhuijsen, S. (2017). 25 years of transparency research: Evidence and future directions. *Public Administration Review*, 77(1), 32–44.

Cucciniello, M., Petracca, F., Ciani, O., & Tarricone, R. (2021). Development features and study characteristics of mobile health apps in the management of chronic conditions: A systematic review of randomised trials. *NPJ Digital Medicine*, 4(1), 144. https://www.nature.com/articles/s41746-021-00517-1.

Cutrona, C. E., Russell, D. W., Hessling, R. M., Brown, P. A., & Murry, V. (2000). Direct and moderating effects of community context on the psychological well-being of African American women. *Journal of Personality and Social Psychology*, 79(6), 1088–1101. https://doi.org/10.1037/0022-3514.79.6.1088.

Déglise, C., Suggs, L. S., & Odermatt, P. (2012). SMS for disease control in developing countries: A systematic review of mobile health applications. *Journal of Telemedicine and Telecare*, 18(5), 273–281.

Delli Carpini, M. X., & Keeter, S. (1996). *What Americans Know about Politics and Why It Matters*. New Heaven, CT: Yale University Press.

Demunter, C., Van Looy, B., & Gemmel, P. (2019). Measuring the impact of service design: The development and validation of a measurement scale. *Journal of Service Management*, 30(3), 326–347.

Design Council. (2007). The double diamond: A universal design process. https://www.designcouncil.org.uk/our-resources/the-double-diamond/.

Dexheimer, J. W., & Borycki, E. M. (2015). mHealth: Revolutionizing healthcare through mobile technologies. *Online Journal of Nursing Informatics*, 19(3), 306–315.

Diana, C., Pacenti, E., & Tassi, R. (2009). *Visualtiles Communication tools for (service) design*. https://servdes.org/pdf/2009/diana-pacenti-tassi.pdf.

Donetto, S., Pierri, P., Tsianakas, V., & Robert, G. (2015). Experience-based Co-design and Healthcare Improvement: Realizing Participatory Design in the Public Sector. *The Design Journal*, 18(2), 227–248. https://doi.org/10.2752/175630615x14212498964312.

Donker, T., Petrie, K., Proudfoot, J. et al. (2013). Smartphones for smarter delivery of mental health programs: A systematic review. *Journal of Medical Internet Research*, 15(11), e247. https://www.jmir.org/2013/11/e247/.

Dorst, K. (2011). The core of "Design Thinking" and its application. *Design Studies*, 32, 521–532. https://doi.org/10.1016/j.destud.2011.07.006.

Downe, L. (2020). *Good Services: How to Design Services that Work*. Amsterdam: Laurence King Publishing.

Dudau, A., Glennon, R., & Verschuere, B. (2019). Co-production as an emerging evidence-based approach in the public sector: A systematic review. *International Journal of Public Sector Management*, 32(2), 182–202.

Dunleavy, P., & Hood, C. (1994). From old public administration to new public management. *Public Money & Management*, 14(3), 9–16.

Edvardsson, B. (2005). Service quality: Beyond cognitive assessment. *Managing Service Quality*, 15, 127–131. 10.1108/09604520510585316.

Edvardsson, B., & Roos, I. (2001). Critical incident techniques. *International Journal of Service Industry Management*, 12(3), 251–268. https://doi.org/10.1108/eum0000000005520.

Edvardsson, B,. Tronvoll, B., & Gruber, T. (2011). Expanding understanding of service exchange and value co-creation: A social construction approach. *Journal of the Academy of Marketing Science*, 39, 327–339. 10.1007/s11747-010-0200-y.

Fagherazzi, G., Goetzinger, C., Rashid, M. A., Aguayo, G. A., & Huiart, L. (2020). Digital health strategies to fight COVID-19 worldwide: Challenges, recommendations, and a call for papers. *Journal of Medical Internet Research*, 16 June; 22(6), e19284. https://www.jmir.org/2020/6/e19284/.

Farr, M. (2018). Power dynamics and collaborative mechanisms in co-production and co-design processes. *Critical Social Policy*, 38(4), 623–644.

Fitzsimmons, J., & Fitzsimmons, M. (2004). *Service Management Operations, Strategy, Information Technology Seventh Edition*. McGraw-Hill Irwin, [online] https://industri.fatek.unpatti.ac.id/wp-content/uploads/2019/03/272-Service-Management-Operations-Strategy-Information-Technology-James-A.-Fitzsimmons-Mona-J.-Fitzsimmons-Edisi-7-2010.pdf.

Funck, E. K., & Karlsson, M. (2020). Rethinking public service delivery: Managing with external providers. *Public Administration Review*, 80(4), 621–630.

Fung, A. (2015). Putting the public back into governance: The challenges of citizen participation and its future. *Public Administration Review*, 75(4), 513–522.

Gascó-Hernández, M., & Torres-Coronas, T. (2015). *Digital Public Administration and E-government in Developing Nations: Policy and Practice*. Hershey, PA: IGI Global.

Gil-Garcia, J. R., Chengalur-Smith, I., & Duchessi, P. (2014). Collaborative e-government: Impediments and benefits of information-sharing projects in the public sector. *European Journal of Information Systems*, 23(2), 123–133.

Glushko, R. J. (2010). Service science: Toward a smarter planet. In *Introduction to Service Engineering* (pp. 3–30). Hoboken, NJ: Wiley.

Goodwin, K. (2009). *Designing for the Digital Age: How to Create Human-Centered Products and Services*. Indianapolis, IN: Wiley.

Grönroos, C. (2016). Internationalization strategies for services: A retrospective. *Journal of Services Marketing*, 30, 129–132. 10.1108/JSM-11-2015-0354.

Grönroos, C. (2019). Reforming public services: Does service logic have anything to offer? *Public Management Review, Taylor & Francis Journals*, 21(5, May), 775–788.

Gronroos, C., & Voima, P. (2013). Critical service logic: Making sense of value creation and co-creation. *Journal of the Academy of Marketing Science*, 41(2), 133–150.

Gummesson, E. (2006). Qualitative research in management: Addressing complexity, context, and persona. *Management Decision*, 44(2), 167–179.

Gustafson, D. H., McTavish, F. M., Chih, M. Y. et al. (2015). A smartphone application to support recovery from alcoholism: A randomized clinical trial. *JAMA Psychiatry*, 72(5), 566–572.

Hardyman, W., Garner, S., Lewis, J. J. et al. (2021). Enhancing public service innovation through value co-creation: Capacity building and the 'innovative imagination'. *Public Money & Management*, 42(5), 1–9. https://doi.org/10.1080/09540962.2021.1981042.

Hardyman, W., Kitchener, M., & Daunt, K. L. (2019). What matters to me! User conceptions of value in specialist cancer care. *Public Management Review*, 21(11), 1687–706. https://doi.org/10.1080/14719037.2019.1619808.

Haveri, A. (2006). Complexity in local government change: Limits to rational reforming. *Public Management Review*, 8(1), 31–46.

Haug, N., Dan, S., & Mergel, I. (2023). Digitally-induced change in the public sector: A systematic review and research agenda. *Public Management Review*, 26(7), 1963–1987. https://doi.org/10.1080/14719037.2023.2234917

Hill-Kayser, C. E., Vachani, C., Hampshire, M. K., Di Lullo, G., & Metz, J. M. (2009). Impact of Internet use on health-related behaviors and the patient-physician relationship: A survey-based study and review. *Journal of Oncology Practice*, 5(6), 281–285.

Hodgkinson, I. R., Hannibal, C., Keating, B. W., Chester Buxton, R., & Bateman, N. (2017). Toward a public service management: Past, present, and future directions. *Journal of Service Management*, 28(5), 998–1023. https://doi.org/10.1108/josm-01-2017-0020.

Holbein, J. B. (2016). Childhood skill development and adult political participation. *American Political Science Review*, 110(3), 572–583.

Holman, H., & Lorig, K. (2000). Patients as partners in managing chronic disease. *British Medical Journal*, 320(7234), 526–527.

Hood, C. (1991). A public management for all seasons? *Public Administration*, 69(1), 3–19.

Howlett, M. (2014). From the 'old' to the 'new' policy design: Design thinking beyond markets and collaborative governance. *Policy Science*, 47, 187–207. https://doi.org/10.1007/s11077-014-9199-0.

Howlett, M., Mukherjee, I., & Woo, J. J. (2015). From tools to toolkits in policy design studies: The new design orientation towards policy formulation research. *Policy & Politics*, 43(2), 291–311. www.designcouncil.org.uk/our-resources/the-double-diamond/.

Huckvale, K., & Car, J. (2014). mHealth app usability problems can limit their effectiveness. *Clinical Pharmacology & Therapeutics*, 95(5), 465–466.

IDEO.org. (2015). *The Field Guide to Human-Centered Design*. San Francisco, CA: IDEO.

Ivankova, N. V., Creswell, J. W., & Stick, S. L. (2006). Using mixed-methods sequential explanatory design: From theory to practice. *Field Methods*, 18(1), 3–20. https://doi.org/10.1177/1525822X05282260.

Jaakkola, E., Helkkula, A., & Aarikka-Stenroos, L. (2015). Understanding and advancing service experience co-creation. *Journal of Service Management*, 26(2). https://doi.org/10.1108/josm-02-2015-0045. https://publichealth.jmir.org/2024/1/e46737.

Jensen, R. E., Duncombe, P., Lai, J. S., & DasMahapatra, P. (2016). Use of electronic patient-reported outcome measures in registered clinical trials: Evidence from ClinicalTrials.gov. *Contemporary Clinical Trials*, 49, 1–6.

Johnston, R., Shulver, M., Slack, N., & Calrk, G. (2020). *Service Operations Management: Improving Service Delivery*. New York: Pearson.

Joiner, K. A., & Lusch, R. F. (2016). Evolving to a new service-dominant logic for health care. *Innovation and Entrepreneurship in Health*, 3, 25–33.

Junginger, S., & Sangiorgi, D. (2009). Service design and organizational change: Bridging the gap between rigour and relevance. *Proceedings of the 3rd Service Design and Service Innovation Conference, ServDes.2010*.

Karpen, I. O., Gemser, G., & Calabretta, G. (2017). A multilevel consideration of service design conditions: Towards a portfolio of organisational capabilities, interactive practices and experiential outcomes. *Journal of Service Theory and Practice*, 27(2), 384–407.

Kim, J., & Lee, C. (2017). An integrated adoption model of mobile cloud services: Exploration of key determinants and extension of technology acceptance model. *Telematics and Informatics*, 34(4), 729–740.

Kimbell, L. (2011). Designing for service as one way of designing services. *International Journal of Design*, 5(2), 41–52.

Kimbell, L., & V. P. Seidel. 2008. *Designing for Services – Multidisciplinary Perspectives*. Oxford: University of Oxford.

King, N. (1998). Template analysis. In G. Symon & C. Cassell (Eds.), *Qualitative Methods and Analysis in Organizational Research: A Practical Guide* (pp. 118–134). London: Sage.

Knapp, M. (1984). *The Economics of Social Care*. London: Macmillan Education.

Krueger, R. A., & Casey, M. A. (2014). *Focus Groups: A Practical Guide for Applied Research* (5th ed.). Thousand Oaks, CA: Sage.

Le Dantec, C. A., & Fox, S. (2015). Strangers at the gate: Gaining access, building rapport, and co-constructing community-based research. *Proceedings of the ACM Conference on Human Factors in Computing Systems (CHI)*, 3797–3806.

Légaré, F., & Witteman, H. O. (2013). Shared decision making: Examining key elements and barriers to adoption into routine clinical practice. *Health Affairs*, 32(2), 276–284.

LoPresti, M., Abraham, O., & Vest, J. R. (2015). A framework for evaluating mHealth implementation and its application to diabetes management. *The American Journal of Managed Care*, 21(11), e623–e630.

Lusch, R. F., & Vargo, S. L. (2006). Service-dominant logic: Reactions, reflections and refinements. *Marketing Theory*, 6(3), 281–288.

Mahmood, S., Hasan, K., Colder Carras, M., & Labrique, A. 2020. Global preparedness against COVID-19: We must leverage the power of digital health. *JMIR Public Health Surveill*, 16 April; 6(2), e18980. https://publichealth.jmir.org/2020/2/e18980/.

Manzini, E., & Jegou, F. (2003). *Sustainable Everyday: Scenarios of Urban Life*. Milano: Edizioni Ambiente.

Martin, L. H., Lassman, D. S., Whittle, J., & Catlin, A. (2012). Recession contributes to slowest annual rate of increase in health spending in five decades. *Health Affairs*, 31(1), 208–219.

Mayer, D. K., Nekhlyudov, L., Snyder, C. F. et al. (2014). American society of clinical oncology clinical expert statement on cancer survivorship care planning. *Journal of Oncology Practice*, 10(6), 345–351.

McCarthy, D., Ryan, J., & Klein, S. (2015). Models of care for high-need, high-cost patients: An evidence synthesis. *The Commonwealth Fund*, 31, 1–19.

McColl-Kennedy, J. R., Vargo, S. L., Dagger, T. S., Sweeney, J. C., & van Kasteren, Y. (2012). Health care customer value cocreation practice styles. *Journal of Service Research*, 15(4), 370–389.

McGann, S., Blomkamp, E., & Lewis, J. M. (2018). The rise of public sector innovation labs: Experiments in design thinking for policy. *Policy Sciences*, 51(3), 249–267.

McTavish, F. M., Chih, M. Y., Shah, D., & Gustafson, D. H. (2015). How patients recovering from alcoholism use a smartphone intervention. *Journal of Dual Diagnosis*, 11(1), 50–57.

Mele, V., & Belardinelli, P. (2018). Mixed methods in public administration research: Selecting, sequencing, and connecting. *Journal of Public Administration Research and Theory. 29*, 10.1093/jopart/muy046.

Meijer, A., & Bolívar, M. P. R. (2016). Governing the smart city: A review of the literature on smart urban governance. *International Review of Administrative Sciences*, 82(2), 392–408.

Mergel, I., Bellé, N., & Nasi, G. (2021). Prosocial motivation of private sector IT professionals joining government. *Review of Public Personnel Administration*, 41(2), 338–357.

Meroni, A., & Sangiorgi, D. (2011). *Design for Services*. Gower.

Miah, S., & Mckay, J. (2014). *A New Conceptualisation Of Design Science Research For DSS Development*. https://vuir.vu.edu.au/30736/1/PACIS%202016%20final%20camera%20ready%20manuscript%20Final.pdf [Accessed 21 March 2024].

Micacchi, M., Cucciniello, M., Trivellato, B., Cristofoli, D., Turrini, A., Valotti, G., & Nasi, G. (2025). How to organize in turbulence: arrangements and pathways for robust governance. *Journal of Public Administration Research and Theory*, 35(2), 231–247.

Miles, M. B., & Huberman, M. A. (1994). *Qualitative Data Analysis: An Expanded Sourcebook* (2nd ed.). Thousand Oaks: Sage.

Millard, J. (2017). Technology innovations in public service delivery for sustainable development. *Public Administration and Information Technology*, 32, 241–282. https://doi.org/10.1007/978-3-319-63743-3_10.

Miller, K. D., Siegel, R. L., Lin, C. C. et al. (2016). Cancer treatment and survivorship statistics, 2016. *CA: A Cancer Journal for Clinicians*, 66(4), 271–289.

Mills, D., Cucciniello, M., Keast, R., Nabatchi, T., & Verleye, K. (2023). Evaluating and extending public service logic–introduction to the special issue. *Public Management Review*, 1–9. https://www.researchgate.net/publication/376024225_Evaluating_and_extending_public_service_logic_-_introduction_to_the_special_issue.

Min, Y. H., Lee, J. W., Shin, Y. W. et al. (2014). Daily collection of self-reporting sleep disturbance data via a smartphone app in breast cancer patients receiving chemotherapy: A feasibility study. *Journal of Medical Internet Research*, 16(5), e135.

Moynihan, D. P., Herd, P., & Harvey, H. (2015). Administrative burden: Learning, psychological, and compliance costs in citizen-state interactions. *Journal of Public Administration Research and Theory*, 25(1), 43–69.

Mulder, S., & Yaar, Z. (2007). Approaches to Creating Personas. *The User Is Always Right: A Practical Guide to Creating and Using Personas for the Web*. Berkeley, CA: New Riders, 33–54.

Mulgan, G., Tucker, S., Ali, R., & Sanders, B. (2007). Social innovation: What it is, why it matters and how it can be accelerated. *Skoll Centre for Social Entrepreneurship*.

Nabatchi, T., Sancino, A., & Sicilia, M. (2017). Varieties of participation in public services: The who, when, and what of coproduction. *Public Administration Review*, 77, 766–776. https://doi.org/10.1111/puar.12765

Nankervis, A., Miyamoto, Y., Taylor, R., & Milton-Smith, J. (2005). *Managing Services*. Cambridge: Cambridge University Press.

Nasi, G., & Choi, Y. (2023). Public administration and the challenge of co-design: Towards a more participatory governance. *Public Management Review*, 25(1), 1–20.

Nasi, G., & Choi, H. 2023 Design strategies for citizen strategic orientation. *Public Management Review*, 1–20.

Nasi, G., Choi, H., Cucciniello, M., & Christensen, R. K. (2023). A systematic literature review of city competitiveness: A 30-year assessment and future agenda for public administration. *Public Management Review*, 25(8), 1562–1586.

Nasi, G., Cucciniello, M., & Guerrazzi, C. (2015). The role of mobile technologies in health care processes: The case of cancer support. *Journal of Medical Internet Research*, 17(2), e26. https://www.jmir.org/2015/2/e26/.

Nasi, G., Osborne, S., Cucciniello, M., & Cui, T. (2024). *Public Service Explained: The Role of Citizens in Value Creation*. Cambridge: Cambridge University Press.

National Cancer Institute.(2023). SEER Cancer Statistics Review. https://seer.cancer.gov/statfacts/html/lungb.html.

Osborne, S. P. (2010). *The New Public Governance? Emerging Perspectives on the Theory and Practice of Public Governance*. Abingdon: Routledge.

Osborne, S. (2020). *Public Service Logic: Creating Value for Public Service Users, Citizens, and Society Through Public Service Delivery* (1st ed.). Routledge. https://doi.org/10.4324/9781003009153.

Osborne, S., Cucciniello, M., & Cui, T. (2024). Public Service Logic: A service lens on the COVID-19 vaccination programmes. In E. Elgar (Ed.), *Research Handbook on Public Management and COVID-19* (pp. 112–125). Cheltenham: Edward Elgar.

Osborne, S. P., Cucciniello, M., Nasi, G., & Strokosch, K. (2021). New development: Strategic user orientation in public services delivery – the missing link in the strategic trinity? *Public Money & Management*, 41(2), 172–175.

Osborne, S. P., Cucciniello, M., Nasi, G., & Zhu, E. (2022). Digital transformation, artificial intelligence and effective public services: challenges and opportunities. *Global Public Policy and Governance*, 2(4), 377–380.

Osborne, S. P., Cucciniello, M., Nasi, G., & Zhu, E. (2022a). Digital transformation, artificial intelligence and effective public services: Challenges and opportunities. *Global Public Policy and Governance*, 2(4), 377–380.

Osborne, S., Powell, M., Cucciniello, M., & Macfarlane, J. (2022b). It is a relay not a sprint! Evolving co-design in a digital and virtual environment: Neighbourhood services for elders. *Global Public Policy and Governance*, 2(4), 518–538.

Osborne, S. P., Radnor, Z., Kinder, T., & Vidal, I. (2014). Sustainable public service organisations: A Public Service-Dominant approach. *Society and Economy*, 36(3), 313–338.

Osborne, S. P., Radnor, Z., & Nasi, G. (2013). A new theory for public service management? Toward a (public) service-dominant approach. *The American Review of Public Administration*, 43(2), 135–158.

Osborne, S. P., Radnor, Z., & Strokosch, K. (2016). Co-production and the co-creation of value in public services: A suitable case for treatment? *Public Management Review*, 18(5), 639–653. https://doi.org/10.1080/14719037.2015.1111927.

Osborne, S. P. and Strokosch, K. (2013). It takes two to tango? *British Journal of Management*, 24, S31–S47. https://doi.org/10.1111/1467-8551.12010.

Osborne, S. P., & Strokosch, K. (2022). Co-production and the co-creation of value in public services: A suitable case for treatment? *Public Management Review*, 24(1), 1–18.

Ostrom, A. Bitner, M., Brown, S., et al. (2010). Moving forward and making a difference: Research priorities for the science of service. *Journal of Service Research* 13, 4–36. 10.1177/1094670509357611.

Osborne, S. P. (2018). From public service-dominant logic to public service logic: Are public service organizations capable of co-production and value co-creation? *Public Management Review*, 20(2), 225–231. https://doi.org/10.1080/14719037.2017.1350461.

Palliative Care Definitions. (n.d.). *World Health Organization.* www.who.int/cancer/palliative/definition/en/.

Petracca, F., Ciani, O., Cucciniello, M., & Tarricone, R. (2020). Harnessing digital health technologies during and after the COVID-19 pandemic: Context matters. *Journal of Medical Internet Research*, 22(12), e21815. https://pubmed.ncbi.nlm.nih.gov/33351777/.

Patrício, L., Fisk, R. P., & Cunha, J. F. e. (2008). Designing multi-interface service experiences: The service experience blueprint. *Journal of Service Research*, 10, 318–334. 10.1177/1094670508314264.

Patrício, L., Fisk, R., Cunha, J. F. e., & Constantine, L. (2011). Multilevel service design: From customer value constellation to service experience blueprint. *Journal of Service Research*, 14, 180–200. 10.1177/1094670511401901.

Popli, S., & Rishi, B. (2021). *Crafting Customer Experience Strategy.* Emerald Group Publishing.

Porumbescu, G. A., Cucciniello, M., Bellé, N., & Nasi, G. (2021). Only hearing what they want to hear: Assessing when and why performance information triggers intentions to coproduce. *Public Administration,* 99(4), 789–802.

Porumbescu, G. A., Piotrowski, S. J., & Mabillard, V. (2021). The impact of transparency on public trust: A cross-national comparative experiment. *Public Administration Review,* 81(2), 206–216.

Prahalad, C. K., & Ramaswamy, V. (2004). Co-creation experiences: The next practice in value creation. *Journal of Interactive Marketing,* 18(3), 5–14.

Prat, N., Comyn-Wattiau, I., & Akoka, J. (2015). A taxonomy of evaluation methods for information systems artifacts. *Journal of Management Information Systems,* 32(3), 229–267. https://doi.org/10.1080/07421222.2015.1099390.

Prestes Joly, M., Teixeira, J. G., Patrício, L., & Sangiorgi, D. (2019). Leveraging service design as a multidisciplinary approach to service innovation. *Journal of Service Management,* 30(6), 681–715. https://doi.org/10.1108/josm-07-2017-0178.

Pruitt, J., & Adlin, T. (2006). *The Persona Lifecycle: Keeping People in Mind Throughout Product Design.* San Francisco, CA: Morgan Kaufmann.

Rajan, B., Tezcan, T., & Seidmann, A. (2019). Service systems with heterogeneous customers: Investigating the effect of telemedicine on chronic care. *Management Science,* 65(4), 1748–1768.

Reason, B., Løvlie, L., & Flu, M. (2015). *Why Service Design.* 10.1002/9781119176541.ch1.

Recker, J., & Mendling, J. (2016). The state of the art of business process management research as published in the BPM Conference: Recommendations for progressing the field. *Business & Information Systems Engineering,* 58(1), 55–72.

Reiter, R., & Klenk, T. (2019). Public governance as co-creation: A strategic framework. *Public Management Review,* 21(11), 1595–1619.

Rose, J., Persson, J. S., Heeager, L. T., & Irani, Z. (2015). Managing e-Government: Value positions and relationships. *Information Systems Journal,* 25(5), 531–571.

Sampson, S. E. (2000). Customer-supplier duality and bidirectional supply chains in service organizations. *International Journal of Service Industry Management,* 11(4), 348–364.

Sanders, R. E. (2005). Validating 'observations' in discourse studies: A methodological reason for attention to cognition. In H. te Molder & J.

Potter (Eds.), *Conversation and Cognition* (pp. 57–78). Cambridge University Press. https://doi.org/10.1017/CBO9780511489990.003.

Sanders, E., & Dandavate, U. (1999). *Design for experiencing: New tools*. TU Delft.

Sanders, E. B.-N., & Stappers, P. J. (2005). Co-creation and the new landscapes of design. *CoDesign*, 4(1), 5–18.

Sanders, E. B.-N., & Stappers, P. J. (2008). Co-creation and the new landscapes of design. *CoDesign*, 4(1), 5–18. https://doi.org/10.1080/15710880701875068.

Sangiorgi, D., & Prendiville, A. (2017). A theoretical framework for studying service design practices: Towards a service ecosystem perspective. *Design Journal*, 20(sup1), S1620–S1635.

Scherer, A., Wünderlich, N. V., & von Wangenheim, F. (2015). The value of self-service: Long-term effects of technology-based self-service usage on customer retention. *MIS Quarterly*, 39(1), 177–200.

Schwoerer, B., Kuehnl, C., & Kuester, S. (2022). Enhancing service design: The role of actor engagement in the service development process. *Journal of Service Management*, 33(4–5), 507–529.

The Scottish Government. (2019). The Scottish Approach to Service Design (SAtSD). Retrieved from https://www.gov.scot/publications/the-scottish-approach-to-service-design/pages/maturity-assessment-matrix/.

Secchi, R., Roth, A. V., & Secchi, E. (2019). *Service Operations Management: Improving Service Delivery* (4th ed.). Harlow: Prentice Hall.

Secomandi, F., & Snelders, D. (2011). The object of service design. *Design Issues*, 27(3), 20–34.

Segelström, F. (2009). *Communicating through Visualizations Service Designers on Visualizing User Research. Paper presented at the 1st Nordic Conference on Service Design and Service Innovation*, Oslo, Norway. – References – Scientific Research Publishing. [online] www.scirp.org. www.scirp.org/reference/referencespapers?referenceid=2018050 [Accessed 21 March 2024].

Senot, C. (2019). The impact of health information technology on patient outcomes: A review and synthesis of the literature. *Journal of Health Organization and Management*, 33(1), 185–207.

Shim, D. C., & Park, H. M. (2016a). Analyzing the determinants of individual action on climate change by specifying belief structures of efficacy and risk. *Policy Sciences*, 49(1), 95–117.

Shim, J., & Park, J.-H. (2016b). Public participation and trust in government: The case of the Korean Financial Regulatory Agency. *Public Performance & Management Review*, 40(1), 1–22. https://doi.org/10.1080/15309576.2016.1177554.

Shostack, G. L. (1982). How to design a service. *European Journal of Marketing*, 16(1), 49–63.

Shostack, L. (1984). *Designing Services That Deliver*. [online] Harvard Business Review. https://hbr.org/1984/01/designing-services-that-deliver.

Simon, H. A. (1969). *The Sciences of the Artificial*. Cambridge, MA: MIT Press.

Singh, S., Drouin, K., Newmark, L. P. et al. (2016). Many mobile health apps target high-need, high-cost populations, but gaps remain. *Health Affairs*, 35(12), 2310–2318.

Sparks, B. (2001). The role of service research in the hospitality literature: An interdisciplinary and international perspective. *International Journal of Hospitality Management*, 20(1), 1–17.

Spruijt-Metz, D., Hekler, E., Saranummi, N. et al. (2015). Building new computational models to support health behavior change and maintenance: New opportunities in behavioral research. *Translational Behavioral Medicine*, 5(3), 335–346. https://doi.org/10.1007/s13142-015-0324-1.

Steen, M., Manschot, M. A. J., & De Koning, N. (2011). Benefits of co-design in service design projects. *International Journal of Design*, 5(2), 53–60. http://resolver.tudelft.nl/uuid:eefaaa3c-cc7d-408e-9e00-883c6f2ccb03.

Stewart, D. M., & Chase, R. B. (1999). The impact of human resource management practices on the performance of firm-customer encounters. *Service Science*, 1(1), 42–58.

Stickdorn, M., Hormess, M. E., Lawrence, A., & Schneider, J. (2018). *This Is Service Design Doing: Applying Service Design Thinking in the Real World*. Sebastopol, CA: O'Reilly Media.

Stickdorn, M., & Schneider, J. (2010). *This Is Service Design Thinking: Basics, Tools, Cases*. Amsterdam: BIS Publishers.

Strandbygaard, U., Thomsen, S. F., & Backer, V. (2010). A daily SMS reminder increases adherence to asthma treatment: A three-month follow-up study. *Respiratory Medicine*, 104(2), 166–171.

Steen, M. (2013). Co-design as a process of joint inquiry and imagination. *Design Issues*. 29, 16–28. 10.1162/DESI_a_00207.

Stentz, J., Clark, V., & Matkin, G. (2012). Applying mixed methods to leadership research: A review of current practices. *The Leadership Quarterly*. 23, 10.1016/j.leaqua.2012.10.001.

Street Jr, R. L., Makoul, G., Arora, N. K., & Epstein, R. M. (2009). How does communication heal? Pathways linking clinician–patient communication to health outcomes. *Patient Education and Counseling*, 74(3), 295–301.

Strokosch, K., & Osborne, S. P. (2020). Co-experience, co-production and co-governance: An ecosystem approach to the analysis of value creation. *Policy & Politics*, 48(3), 425–442.

Strokosch, K., & Osborne, S. P. (2023). Design of services or designing for service? The application of design methodology in public service settings. *Policy & Politics*, 51(2), 1–19. https://doi.org/10.1332/030557321x16750746455167.

Sundberg, K., Wengström, Y., Blomberg, K. et al. (2017). Early detection of symptoms and self-care strategies in ovarian cancer. *European Journal of Oncology Nursing*, 29, 22–28.

Sweeney, J. C., Danaher, T. S., McColl-Kennedy, J. R., & Lévesque, T. J. (2015). Customer effort in value cocreation activities: Improving quality of life and behavioral intentions of health care customers. *Journal of Service Research*, 18(3), 318–335.

Tarricone, R., Cucciniello, M., Armeni, P. et al. (2019). Mobile health divide between clinicians and patients in cancer care: Results from a cross-sectional international survey. *JMIR mHealth and uHealth*, 7(9), e13584. https://pubmed.ncbi.nlm.nih.gov/31493318/.

Teddlie, C., & Tashakkori, A. (2006). A general typology of research designs featuring mixed methods. *Research in the Schools*, 13(1), 12–28.

Tremblay, M. C., Hevner, A. R., & Berndt, D. J. (2010a). Exploratory and confirmatory focus groups in qualitative inquiry. *Qualitative Health Research*, 20(12), 1660–1671.

Tremblay, M. C., Hevner, A. R., & Berndt, D. J. (2010b). Focus groups for artifact refinement and evaluation in design research. *Communications of the Association for Information Systems*, 26, Article 27. https://scispace.com/pdf/focus-groups-for-artifact-refinement-and-evaluation-in-u9mcm31fwg.pdf.

Tremblay, M. C., Hevner, A. R., & Berndt, D. J. (2012). Design of an information volatility measure for health care decision making. *Decision Support Systems*, 52(2), 331–341. https://doi.org/10.1016/j.dss.2011.08.009.

Trischler, J., Dietrich, T., & Rundle-Thiele, S. (2019). Co-design: From expert- to user-driven ideas in public service design. *Public Management Review*, 21(11), 1595–1619.

Trischler, J., Pervan, S. J., Kelly, S. J., & Scott, D. R. (2018). The value of codesign: The effect of customer involvement in service design teams. *Journal of Service Research*, 21(1), 75–100.

Trischler, J., Røhnebæk, M., Edvardsson, B., & Tronvoll, B. (2023). Advancing Public Service Logic: Moving towards an ecosystemic framework for value creation in the public service context. *Public Management Review*, 1–29. https://doi.org/10.1080/14719037.2023.2229836.

Trischler, J., & Scott, D. R. (2015). Designing public services: The usefulness of three service design methods for identifying user experiences. *Public Management Review*, 18(5), 718–739. https://doi.org/10.1080/14719037.2015.1028017.hi.

Trischler, J., & Trischler, J. (2020). The role of the physical environment in co-designing public services. *Public Management Review*, 22(12), 1763–1782.

Turner-McGrievy, G. M., Davidson, C. R., Wingard, E. E., Wilcox, S., & Frongillo, E. A. (2015). Comparative effectiveness of plant-based diets for weight loss: A randomized controlled trial of five different diets. *Nutrition (Burbank, Los Angeles County, Calif.)*, 31(2), 350–358. https://doi.org/10.1016/j.nut.2014.09.002.

Uhm, K. E., Yoo, J. S., Chung, S. H. et al. (2017). Effects of exercise intervention in breast cancer survivors: A meta-analysis of 33 randomized controlled trails. *Oncology Nursing Forum*, 44(3), E105–E115.

van Aken, J. E., Chandrasekaran, A., & Halman, J. I. (2016). Conducting and publishing design science research: Inaugural essay of the design science department of the Journal of Operations Management. *Journal of Operations Management*, 47–48, 1–8.

van Buuren, A., Lewis, J. M., Guy Peters, B., & Voorberg, W. (2020). Improving public policy and administration: Exploring the potential of design. *Policy & Politics*, 48(1), 3–19. https://doi.org/10.1332/030557319x15579230420063.

Van Ryzin, G. G. (2015). The measurement of overall satisfaction. *Public Performance & Management Review*, 39(1), 169–193.

Vargo, S. L. (2008). Customer integration and value creation: Paradigmatic traps and perspectives. *Journal of Service Research*, 11(2), 211–215.

Vargo, S. L., & Akaka, M. A. (2012). Value cocreation and service systems (re)formation: A service ecosystems view. *Service Science*, 4(3), 207–217.

Vargo, S. L., & Lusch, R. F. (2004). Evolving to a new dominant logic for marketing. *Journal of Marketing*, 68(1), 1–17.

Vargo, S. L., & Lusch, R. F. (2008). Service-dominant logic: Continuing the evolution. *Journal of the Academy of Marketing Science*, 36(1), 1–10.

Vargo, S. L., & Lusch, R. F. (2016). Institutions and axioms: An extension and update of service-dominant logic. *Journal of the Academy of Marketing Science*, 44, 5–23. https://doi.org/10.1007/s11747-015-0456-3.

Vargo, S. L., & Lusch, R. F. (2017). Service-dominant logic 2025. *International Journal of Research in Marketing*, 34, 46–67. https://doi.org/10.1016/j.ijresmar.2016.11.001.

Vargo, S. L., Maglio, P. P., & Akaka, M. A. (2008). On value and value co-creation: A service systems and service logic perspective. *European Management Journal*, 26(3), 145–152.

Vink, J., Koskela-Huotari, K., Tronvoll, B., Edvardsson, B., & Wetter-Edman, K. (2021a). Service ecosystem design: Propositions, process model, and future research agenda. *Journal of Service Research*, 24(2), 168–186. https://doi.org/10.1177/1094670520952537.

Vink, J., Wetter-Edman, K., & Koskela-Huotari, K. (2021b). Designerly approaches for catalyzing change in social systems: A social structures approach. *She Ji The Journal of Design Economics and Innovation.* 7, 242–261. 10.1016/j.sheji.2020.12.004.

von Hippel, E. (1994). "Sticky Information" and the Locus of Problem Solving: Implications for Innovation. *Management Science*, 40(4), 429-439.

Voorberg, W. H., Bekkers, V. J. J. M., & Tummers, L. G. (2015). A systematic review of co-creation and co-production: Embarking on the social innovation journey. *Public Management Review*, 17(9), 1333–1357.

Wetter-Edman, K., Sangiorgi, D., Edvardsson, B. et al. (2014). Design for value co-creation: Exploring synergies between design for service and service logic. *Service Science*, 6(2), 106–121. https://doi.org/10.1287/serv.2014.0068.

Whicher, A., & Trick, L. (2019). *Design for Public Good.* London: Design Council.

World Cancer Research Fund/American Institute for Cancer Research. (2017). Continuous Update Project Expert Report 2018. Diet, nutrition, physical activity, and lung cancer. www.wcrf.org/dietandcancer/lung-cancer.

World Health Organization. (2016). mHealth: New horizons for health through mobile technologies. *Global Observatory for eHealth series – Volume 3.* World Health Organization.

World Health Organization. (2018). Cancer fact sheets: Lung cancer. www.who.int/news-room/fact-sheets/detail/cancer.

Young, M. M. (2021). The impact of technological innovation on service delivery: Social media and smartphone integration in a 311 system. *Public Management Review*, 24(6), 1–25. https://doi.org/10.1080/14719037.2021.1877794.

Young, O. R. (2022). Governance in the digital age: A research agenda. *Policy Sciences*, 55(1), 143–155.

Yu, E., & Sangiorgi, D. (2018). Service design as an approach to implement the value co-creation perspective in new service development. *Journal of Service Research*, 21(1), 40–58.

Zeithaml, V. A., Parasuraman, A., & Berry, L. L. (1985). Problems and strategies in services marketing. *Journal of Marketing*, 49(2), 33–46. https://doi.org/10.1177/002224298504900203.

Zomerdijk, L. G., & Voss, C. A. (2010). Service design for experience-centric services. *Journal of Service Research*, 13(1), 67–82.

Cambridge Elements

Public and Nonprofit Administration

Robert Christensen
Brigham Young University
Robert Christensen is the George W. Romney Professor of Public and Nonprofit Management at Brigham Young University.

Jaclyn Piatak
University of North Carolina at Charlotte
Jaclyn Piatak is co-editor of NVSQ and Professor of Political Science and Public Administration at the University of North Carolina at Charlotte.

Rosemary O'Leary
University of Kansas
Rosemary O'Leary is the Edwin O. Stene Distinguished Professor Emerita of Public Administration at the University of Kansas.

About the Series
The foundation of this series are cutting-edge contributions on emerging topics and definitive reviews of keystone topics in public and nonprofit administration, especially those that lack longer treatment in textbook or other formats. Among keystone topics of interest for scholars and practitioners of public and nonprofit administration, it covers public management, public budgeting and finance, nonprofit studies, and the interstitial space between the public and nonprofit sectors, along with theoretical and methodological contributions, including quantitative, qualitative and mixed-methods pieces.

The Public Management Research Association
The Public Management Research Association improves public governance by advancing research on public organizations, strengthening links among interdisciplinary scholars, and furthering professional and academic opportunities in public management.

Cambridge Elements

Public and Nonprofit Administration

Elements in the Series

Redefining Development: Resolving Complex Challenges in a Global Context
Jessica Kritz

Experts in Government: The Deep State from Caligula to Trump and Beyond
Donald F. Kettl

New Public Governance as a Hybrid: A Critical Interpretation
Laura Cataldi

Can Governance be Intelligent?: An Interdisciplinary Approach and Evolutionary Modelling for Intelligent Governance in the Digital Age
Eran Vigoda-Gadot

The Courts and the President: Judicial Review of Presidentially Directed Action
Charles Wise

Standing Up for Nonprofits: Advocacy on Federal, Sector-wide Issues
Alan J. Abramson and Benjamin Soskis

Topics in Public Administration: Perspectives from Computational Social Sciences and Corpus Linguistics
Richard M. Walker, Jiasheng Zhang and Yanto Chandra

Public Service Explained: The Role of Citizens in Value Creation
Greta Nasi, Stephen Osborne, Maria Cucciniello and Tie Cui

Court-Ordered Community Service: The Experiences of Community Organizations and Community Service Workers
Rebecca Nesbit, Su Young Choi and Jody Clay-Warner

Sustainable Inclusion through Performance-Driven Practices: An Evidence-Based, Dynamic Systems Framework
Ruth Sessler Bernstein and Paul Salipante

Bureaucratic Resistance in Times of Democratic Backsliding
João V. Guedes-Neto and B. Guy Peters

Design Strategies in Public Services
Maria Cucciniello, Greta Nasi, Gregory Porumbescu and Rosanna Tarricone

A full series listing is available at: www.cambridge.org/EPNP

For EU product safety concerns, contact us at Calle de José Abascal, 56–1°, 28003 Madrid, Spain or eugpsr@cambridge.org.